Charles B[ukowski]

Selected Letters Volume 3
1971–1986

First published in 2004 by
Virgin Books Ltd
Thames Wharf Studios
Rainville Road
London
W6 9HA

Copyright © Linda Lee Bukowski 1995, 1999

Previously published in the USA by Black Sparrow Press in *Living on Luck* and *Reach for the Sun*

The right of Charles Bukowski to be identified as the Author of this Work has been asserted by him in accordance with the Copyright, Designs and Patents Act, 1988.

This book is sold subject to the condition that it shall not, by way of trade or otherwise, be lent, resold, hired out or otherwise circulated without the publisher's prior written consent in any form of binding or cover other than that in which it is published and without a similar condition including this condition being imposed on the subsequent purchaser.

A catalogue record for this book is available from the British Library.

ISBN 0 7535 0946 6

Typeset by Phoenix Photosetting, Chatham, Kent
Printed and bound in Great Britain by Clays Ltd, St Ives PLC

Editor's Note

This third volume of Bukowski's letters begins in the 1970s. Throughout this decade, as royalties begin to overtake the stipend and he gradually gains confidence that he will be able not merely to survive but to prosper in this new career, the letters return again and again with wonder to his sense of how lucky he is to enjoy being able to live by writing. By the end of the decade, he's the owner of a comfortable house and a new BMW. His worries now are how to protect his fruit trees from frost, how to lower his tax liability, and how to deal with Hollywood directors and stars.

As in volumes 1 and 2, the letters have been selected and transcribed from photocopies furnished by libraries and individuals. Bukowski's correspondence was astonishingly voluminous, and only selections are given from most letters. Editorial omissions are indicated by asterisks in square brackets, thus: [* * *]. Ellipses in the original letters are indicated by three dots. Bukowski often typed in CAPITALS for emphasis or for titles. Here, book titles are printed in *italics*, poem titles in quotes, and emphatic capitals in SMALL CAPS.

Dates are regularized and sometimes supplied from postmarks or guessed at from other evidence. A few spelling errors have been silently corrected. Salutations and signatures are for the most part omitted, except for a few examples that give the characteristic flavor. Some attempt is made to preserve Bukowski's layout, which at times includes multiple margins, but a printed book cannot reproduce such effects unaltered. As in the previous volume, a few letters have been printed verbatim to give the flavor of a completely unedited letter.

Acknowledgments

The editor and publisher thank the following institutions for supplying copies of some of the letters in this volume:

> University of Arizona, Special Collections
> Brown University, Providence, John Hay Library
> The University of California, Los Angeles, Special Collections
> The University of California, Santa Barbara, Special Collections
> Centenary College, Samuel Peters Research Library, Shreveport, Louisiana
> The State University of New York at Buffalo, Poetry/Rare Books Collection
> The University of Southern California, Rare Books Collection
> Temple University Library, Special Collections

• 1971 •

Laugh Literary and Man the Humping Guns, *published by Hatchetman Press, was the literary magazine that Bukowksi edited and published in collaboration with Neeli Cherry from February 1969. It ran for three issues until February 1971.*

[To John Martin]
January 6, 1971

only one poem enclosed, those crayon drawings have drained my ass. went down today to cash a check for one dollar from Univ. of Calif. at Berk. girl looked at deposit book – it said: *Laugh Literary and Man the Humping Guns*; also, Hatchetman Press, she started blushing and giggling . . . "pardon me, sir, can I ask you what this is?" "it's a magazine. as you can see, we are going broke." "o, I think that title's terribly funny, sir." "that's nice. I only wish somebody would buy the magazine. . . ." the girls always react to those titles; they really get heated as if they wanted to be raped.

last time I went one of the girls told me, "O, I think this is so *cool*!" then she walked over and showed it to another girl and then they both heated up.

what the hell. after centuries of magazines being named *Circle* and *Ante* and *Blast* and all that dry grease, we finally break the mould. what happens? First a letter from Blazek, inflamed, claiming that we were corny, exaggerated our purpose, on and on and on and so forth and so forth. what the hell. so what happens? now all the new mags coming out are named like this: *When John Rode His Bicycle West to Fight the Indians*, and so forth and so forth. . . .

anyhow, I took my dollar and walked out of there and came back here, walked into bedroom and here are two women's legs sticking out from under the covers. a dead body! that drunken bitch from . . . I threw the covers back. just 2 legs. my landlord is a very funny man, he's so god damned funny that some day he's going to give somebody a heart attack.

all right, unward, I mean *on*ward and upward and out. . . .

[To Lafayette Young]
Jan 6, 1971

[★ ★ ★] the book I guess will be out soon. I am playing with my little crayons. Look, pal, don't expect a *War and Peace*. well, that's lousy . . . I mean, don't expect another *Journey* by Celine . . . no excuses, shit. I wrote it in 20 drunken nights and I mean *drunken* . . . just a flash of hell. a lifetime shot and nibbled at in a decaying room by a decaying man. I'm not a novelist; it's too much WORK, and so it really isn't a novel. oh, hell.

some girl in her twenties, just out of a madhouse, rather hanging around now and then. I find her *quite* sane, quite lovely . . . especially the color of the eye and the way it looks at me. she's quite nice to me but most women are at the start . . . then they trap you in, and BOOM!!! . . . the wake-up . . . and you think, after all those others, you should have known better . . . men are too adventurous . . . esp. old men like me . . . whiskey, women, horses . . . same old song . . . then you're in the cage, wondering what happened. [★ ★ ★]

Post Office *was printed in January 1971 and officially published on February 8.*

[To John Martin]
January 22, 1971

I sent the ad (flyer) on to *NOLA* and asked that they run it. I guess they will. It should swing some sales. Don't forget to send copy of book to Ben Pleasants. There is a possibility he may review it in the *Times*, though we have no way of knowing. He has tried to run stuff on me before but they always cut it off. But there's a chance. There's definitely an anti-Bukowski thing going on, has been for years. For instance, I'm supposed to read at The Other Side Wednesday night (the 27th) but the dear old *L.A. Free Press* didn't run it in their Calendar section, which means I'll be reading to an empty house, which would be all right with me except the poet gets the entrance fee per head $1.25 minus ten percent. Los Angeles has always been the roughest town on me because I am basically an isolationist . . . well, enough bitching. so I'll have to go through with it anyhow, so leave Wednesday out as a signing day. [★ ★ ★]

Now there's something else going. I didn't get all the names. Katz knows this publisher, so forth. all the letters I've written Jimmy [Pitts], Katz has them. they are locked up in a vault by Katz and no human eye sees them. JESUS! there's your laugh for today. anyhow, the human eyes that have seen them think that they are pretty good, along with those I've written to Lafayette Young, and Katz wants this publisher to run them – *The Letters of Charles Bukowski*. I have an idea that the letters to Jimmy Pitts were not so excellent but those to Lafayette Young, I put something into. I don't know if you ever met L.Y. but he's one of the finest people I've ever met.

So I told Jimmy I'd have to check with John Martin and then he got a little unhappy. So what do you think about this book – proposed book – John, while you're thinking of everything else? Do you have a moment to give me some thoughts on it? [★ ★ ★]

[To Gerald Locklin]
February 8, 1971

[★ ★ ★] Gerald, you can't be an honest man *and* a book reviewer at the same time. Honest men are supposed to write books and salesmen are expected to review them. Of course, not many honest men write books, but you know what I mean. [★ ★ ★]

[To John Martin]
April 7, 1971

back in after battles and love and madness on 2 Arizona ranches . . . haven't heard from Santa Barbara yet. perhaps the stuff is too dirty for them. we shoulda taken the 1500. a bird in the hand.

still trying to put together the book for Ferl[inghetti]. taking too long, I suppose. haven't heard a word from him. heard from Weissner who says Meltzer willing to give $500 advance plus ten percent royalties for *NOLA Express* stories plus *All the Assholes in the World and Mine*. will have to check City Lights contract on foreign rights. the problem is getting the shit to these guys. I've been cutting out the *Nola* stories – slowly – and putting printer's instructions on them. and I only have one copy of each paper. in fact, I even lost one copy with my best story in it – "The White Beard." I don't know what the hell. there aren't enough hours in the day. and after mailing this, I'm going to drive over to Burbank to play around with this woman-woman. maybe I don't know what I'm doing. it seems there has to be time to live, time to write and time to scrounge up materials and answer mail and so forth, type shit, or clip it out. I'm hardly bitching. for I'm still alive and the action is banging the walls, but –

Weissner sends a copy of *twen* (german mag) with reprint of Thurber story. W. says in the introduction to the story they say, "If we weren't sure he would turn it down, we would recommend him for the Literary Nobel Prize." See how the game goes? No wonder writers go to self-love, the way they powder them up. For me, it's pure gamble every time I sit down to this typer. Nothing is ever easy. I never know if I can ever do it again. A man can never call himself a writer; a man is always an x-writer.

like these poems enclosed, I feel that they do not quite shake loose. It's been a bad year so far for my writing. April already. Maybe the juices will explode like mad marmalade? soon?

[To Carl Weissner]
April 10, 1971

have been back in frozen state – not getting any work done. wild hot love affair with beautiful 30 years old sculptress, been going on some months now. I don't know what she wants with an old guy like me but since she's around I give her plenty of ACTION. kind of like trying to hold onto the tail of a female tigress at times, though. she did 3 weeks in a madhouse some years back and she's plenty unpredictable. She just came off a ten year marriage and looking for breathing room. I give her room. But afraid I'm hooked in – her delicious mind, body, et al., and the way she makes love . . . jesus. well. [★ ★ ★]

I'm on the wagon as much as possible because I have to fuck so much now, go down, so forth . . . [★ ★ ★] I was fucking during the earthquake, it simply added to it.

Bukowski, with John Martin's help, had sold his first literary archive — consisting of manuscripts, magazine appearances, and letters to him — to the Library at the University of California, Santa Barbara, for $5,000.

[To John Martin]
April 19, 1971

[★ ★ ★] just 2 poems enclosed. since the luck with Santa Barbara I have decided to take the leisurely approach. the poem must work itself up without whip or bait. there won't be as many but I feel that they will be better. the stories too will probably drift a bit away from the sex motif. for the first time I've felt I can take a breath. I think the writing will be of a higher order. well, we'll see, won't we?

I really feel that I can allow myself to feel good — for a while anyhow. it's a matter of pace and tide and hidden elements. the boogie man is drunk and we have picked his pockets.

fly. why walk?

Charley the yea-sayer

[To Carl Weissner]
April 25, 1971

ass drag from giving shitty poetry readings [★ ★ ★] and also a battle with the tigress for acting like a silly vamp. she doesn't fuck the boys but she just about tickles their balls in front of me. very highschoolgirl stuff, and I'm supposed to react to that by tickling some other gal's cunt. cheap vengeance, you know. fuck, Carl, I been around too long to play children's games. however, at this time, the tigress and I are still mating. for whatever it means. [★ ★ ★]

well, I don't know how poetry does in Germany but Martin phoned that *The Days Run Away* is now going into a *third* printing, which I understand is some kind of record for Black Sparrow. so they do read poetry out here. [★ ★ ★]

Cherry was co-editor of Laugh Literary and Man the Humping Guns.

[To Neeli Cherry]
[mid 1971]

[★ ★ ★] I also enclose the subscription order from the University of Chicago Library. Don't lose it down the envelope, somewhere. I hope you are taking care of these university subscriptions, Neeli! I am busting ass reading this garbage coming in and sending it back. It takes hours and there are more submissions each day.

This Univ. of Chicago thing is easier. They don't ask for the quadruplicate shit. Do your job, kid.

Heard from Bennet who claims he sent a dollar and never got his copy. He was a bit nasty about it. Instead of mailing him a copy, I sent him a dollar and told him to roll it around his Hava-Havana and jam it. Also returned his work which was lousy except for one section. He's the former editor of *Vagabond*, now lives in Frisco in a $175 pad while his wife works for him. He writes, "I'm never going to work again." How do these guys do it? Where do these women come from? That support the halfass and incompetent Artist? ah, shit!!! [★ ★ ★]

[To John Martin]
June [?5], 1971

here it is early June and I'm still batting .189, but I figure if I hit .400 through the rest of the months, the damn things just gotta climb. I believe that slumps are somehow necessary. meanwhile, I look around and notice nobody else is hitting the ball either. [★ ★ ★]

my love life is eating at some of my time but for this you must forgive me. to make writing and life and people work all right is a full time job. luckily, there's no post office. I absorb. I think it will make the writing better. trust my instincts, what the hell. I think about you quite a bit and must realize you think I am fucking off. I am always a student, John. I will die a student. it would be wonderful to continue to survive as I have. you have no idea how things have opened up. torrents rush all over me, man. everything will be there. you know what I mean. [★ ★ ★]

[To John Martin]
[ca. June 19, 1971]

things are difficult, of course. haven't they always been?

Packard (*N.Y. Quarterly*) writes of the poem "A Well-Known Poet and Myself," "Couldn't possibly print this poem of yours as it would blow the whistle on too many of our leading poets."

perhaps he is joking. however, I've often had the feeling that the whole game is jaked-up, jacked-off. o.k., I'm bitching.

listen, kid, who you got in my spot in left field? you know damn well he can't hit a curve off his wrists. soon as they find that out he's gonna go zero for 24 and I'll trot back out there on the green, .287 maybe but good in the clutch, rbi, and when I get a hit it's a hit, I can't run anymore.

I can't run anymore. The fight grows deep. That's the way it should be.

hang in.

[To Carl Weissner]
June 22, 1971

have been backed up in a wake of shit and my own insanity . . . cops by the other night, 2 cops and a citizen carrying a shotgun. the tigress had busted loose but was gone, having left behind bits of glass and broken booze bottles everywhere. these scenes keep occurring, battle after battle and hell, I don't know if it's worth it. even a good piece of ass is only a piece of ass and when the price gets too high you don't pay it. but like she sez, things are never dull when we get together.

[* * *] right now I've got to take out the garbage cans once a week and bring them back, also must drink with the landlord and landlady to hold rent down. what I do for the world of Art, nobody's ever going to understand unless I talk right out and maybe give them a nosebleed on my deathbed. shit, I hope I end up with a bed to die in. [* * *]

[To John Martin]
July 1, 1971

[★ ★ ★] go easy on me and my gal friend. It's painful, of course, but there are benefits. and don't forget Scott had his Zelda.

"listen," I tell her, "you're not going to push my ass around because you're 20 years younger."

"and you're not going to push my ass around because you're a writer," she tells me.

a writer, I think, so that's it. I thot it wuz my good looks.

she'll do a sculpture of you for $200, John. She's pretty good.

I got my sculpture free.

(or so it says here.) [★ ★ ★]

[To Neeli Cherry]
July 12, 1971

for Christ's sake, man, enclosed this order from *Either/Or*. we can get rid of 20 copies. also those ten on that other order — that's 30 copies, that's 18 dollars! that will give us close to 70 bucks and I'm having rough shit with $$$$$. this is REAL MONEY FOR US. WE CAN SPEND IT! think about it. [★ ★ ★]

Hank Malone is a poet living in Detroit.

[To Hank Malone]
July 13, 1971

answering yours NOW of May 4th, this year, which shows my mind-state. god, yes. well, I've always been . . . ????? stacks of paper . . . dirty sheets . . . lost manuscripts . . . beer bottles and shorts under the bed, the blues, the deep down blues. peak of elation. such shit. age, age. the streets. the dirty clouds. well.

as per a "literary conspiracy" against me, I suppose that a great many do hate me — much of it caused by my writing style which is rather unpoetic. also in my drinking moments I have caused difficult feelings, I suppose. no excuses, man. also, in my own short stories I am often the bastard-villain of the pieces. I guess I am convincing. also I don't mingle much with the literatti. literoti, eh? . . . no New York City or North Beach up at Frisco, none of that. I am the loner. people come around here, I beer-up, and I have a tendency to run them out the door. all in all I suppose I have given off rays that I am a son of a bitch. they almost have me believing it myself.

I seem to be surviving, which means writing dirty stories, being lucky and giving a few poetry readings. I don't ask the universities to read, I wait on them, and although I have gotten quite a number of readings I suppose I could get more ??? if I pushed. but I am the bullhead, and so there you go. Univ. of Arkansas made me a recent $300 offer (total) but shit you put in plane fare round trip and all I have left is a used pork chop bone. so I'm waiting for some Univ. near Arkansas to toddle along and make me an offer, which prob. won't happen. I cry the blues, haha.

guy over other night claims this woman is pissed at me. She wrote me from Univ. of Wisconsin offering a year's professorship, claims I didn't even bother to answer her letter. Truth is, I never got the lady's letter and I told the guy I thought it was bullshit and the guy said, she doesn't bullshit, you want her address and I said, no. I just feel it's bullshit. or maybe I want the death-shroud. my god, what's wrong with me?

well, I guess the game will end soon enough. meanwhile I sit by the typer here writing Malone in Detroit, so all hail, and luck, may the power stay on. it is a fight in hell. but not just for the writer. but maybe for the writer it is worse because he keeps the light on, keeps studying the embankments and the snakes and the dogs and the whores and the snails and the people and the streets, and it's all bound to cut in and take a bite now and then, mostly now, and what a game, it's like getting knocked down in the first round, the lights whirling, and there are sounds and you swing, and you're brave and you're a coward, and it's the sound of the typer against everything, and everything's much, and you know this, so hang in, then, hang tough.

[To Carl Weissner]
July 13, 1971

[★ ★ ★] the tigress is in the other room writing a poem, typing a poem about the night both of us went ape-shit. I have two editors and a professor pissed at me. standard procedure. have only made it with one prof, been drunk with him and his wife 3 or 4 times, real easy nights, good talk – one Bix Blaufuss. Also one other prof, one Andre Sedricks, but he was too good a guy – Univ. of Kansas, they let him go, last I heard he was working in a bean factory. [★ ★ ★]

Saw Norse the other night, afternoon. Took tigress over and Norse and tigress talked about Spooks, Visions, Dreams, the Astral Dome of Revelation, man, I was OUT of it, but it was interesting enough. plus I have more or less been on the wagon and I have to learn how to TALK ALL OVER AGAIN WHEN I AM SOBER. I am like a baby trying to find its speech. well, learn learn, you know, that's what keeps the pecker hard.

I read at a poetry benefit for Patchen who lives in Palo Alto. Bad back, sure, yes I know. o.k. but I sat and listened to the poetry and that was bad back too, you know. had to fall off the wagon to maintain sanity. rich guy's house in hills. after the reading was over I served the folk from behind the bar. each drink I served I poured one for myself. don't remember getting on in. but here I am, several days later, looking out the window at DeLongpre . . . tomorrow I take out the garbage cans to help hold down the rent. next day I haul them in. ah, the life of the Poet, sweet Jesus, but it's too late for anything else, I'm too ugly now, too insane, too old, I am just going to have to luck it. and the best luck is to keep this typewriter HOT. yes. [★ ★ ★]

we are hanging in here, we are going to make that siffed-up Papa Death work a bit to get us in the corner. Why not? That fucking coward has been picking on people, animals, flies, buildings, streetcars, stockings, shoelaces and mattresses and birds and flowers and fleas and streets long enough . . .

[To John Martin]
August 2, 1971

    damn, I can't think of a title or titles of proposed book. my head is empty air (smog-filled). I suppose they'll come along. a little list. but sometimes I wonder how you're surviving. all these people who knock on my door are out of jobs. and I sit here playing at being writer. it's very odd. sometimes it feels like a movie I'm watching. girls, booze, phone ringing ... hours of madness ... hours of luxury ... hours to wrestle with like an octopus in a tank. of course, it's going to be defeat, finally. but it's much nicer to be defeated on my grounds than on theirs. very important. almost magic. the magic defeat. meanwhile, the war is still on and here's a couple more poems, old boy.

decidedly yours, Henry Armstrong

[To John Martin]
September 12, 1971

    Thanks for the stamps, big dad, but I see the Waldorf towers a long way off, if ever. A bare survival unto death is my dream. The life I live now is dangerous but good. And I think too that in my second year at it the writing is gluing itself together more. Although the enclosed poems are more comfortable than great, I think a few goodies sit waiting, smoking cigars and talking in the waiting room of my head. And I haven't thought of a title for the next book of poems but will work on it SOON big boss. – oh yes, the sculptress and I split continually; I always think it's over; next thing you know we're back together again. mercy, reason and logic have very little place in my life. great then.

the flying ace, Major Henry

E. V. Griffith had published Bukowski's first book in 1960, Flower, Fist and Bestial Wail. *See volume 1, passim.*

[To E. V. Griffith]
September 27, 1971

The 50 looked good, doctor. I don't know if you know but I quit my job at age 50 . . . a supposedly good civil service gig . . . a couple of years ago and am living on my luck, so all such checks contain an immense spiritual as well as practical lift. Practical in that it allows me to go on and spiritual in the fact that it allows me to go on in the way I want to. I think my writing has upped itself since I quit work; there's more energy and more humor and more life in the lines. But actually, I didn't quit the job for the good of literature, for the good of The Poem, but because the Motherfarting job was really killing me. I was in the doctor's office once or twice a week, one thing or another. I couldn't lift my arms up to my shoulders; my whole body was one mass of pain; white blisters broke out on the tops and bottoms of both hands; dizzy spells . . . man, I was DYING FROM THE UNHAPPINESS OF DOING THE OTHER MAN'S THING FOR 50 YEARS. I suppose a writer is not supposed to be too happy is he? I have moments of great depression now when I think I am going crazy, but I also have hours to LOLL AROUND IN LIKE BEACHWATER, and it fills, man, it fills like sunlight and love. I deserve a small slice of minor contentment; I have it coming; for this moment the gods are letting it come my way. Total suffering without relief is useless.

Then too, the love of the female is more apt to come around when one is rested, when one is a bum, when one is lounging over a typer with coffee and rolled cigarette at 3 in the afternoon, then love is more apt to arrive. Love doesn't like time clocks and some dog giving his guts to a punch press. All I am saying is that things have been mighty damned good . . . meaning I am surviving, I am paying the rent, the child support, the health is bouncing, the love is good . . . I take out the garbage cans and bring them back in to knock ten dollars off the rent. I sleep until noon and go to bed at 2 or 3 a.m. And I've learned to live with that typewriter. I mean, I wait until it's ready, or I think I wait until it's ready. I still write bad stuff but it's all in the flow, in the working, it counts, it helps somehow. Don't get me wrong, the world hasn't changed, and I know I can be out on the street soon enough. I've even gone up on the hill with the bums and taken them beer and beans and crackers and smokes. They live in the trees up there above the freeway. It's green and it's quiet and it's tolerable if anything is tolerable. But there ain't any mailbox up there and you can't very well type or write up there. But the luck is holding. The Black Sparrow books, *Days* and *Post Office* keep going into reprintings and there's a new book of poems coming up, and also Ferlinghetti says there will be a book of short stories soon. I've been lucky in the fact that I haven't gotten famous and rich through, say, a one-shot novel via a big publishing house. The gods have let me go on like this, getting by. It's good for the inner springs, the old gut mattress. It couldn't be planned better if I had chosen the way myself. [★ ★ ★]

[To John Martin]
October 5, 1971

I'm a bit depressed but, then, haven't I always been? I do like these poems, tho, better than the last batch I sent you, but, like you know, maybe out of 50 poems written, maybe one comes through as it should. I have learned to wait more and press less, and I believe that has helped the writing. I now figure that I am *writing* when I am doing nothing and that it takes a lot of doing nothing in order to write. What I mean is, that sorting mail while waiting is destructive; doing nothing is doing something . . . we learn so slowly and when we've almost learned it all, it's about too late.

I wanted to enclose the letter from this editor saying that Creeley stated that I was the only poet that he disliked, but can't find it. I'm plenty up on Creeley, I almost dislike all the poets. But, then, he's intelligent. [★ ★ ★]

[To Steve Richmond]
November 5, 1971

sure, o.k. on *Laugh*. outa sentimentality I'd like to see it go an issue or 2 more. I think our covers were the most immortal part of the magazine, but–. also, we lost our files. that is, the subscribers and libraries, and when we had them, our good friend N[eeli] ignored them. the only way I know about them is when they write us. I am trying to fill some orders now. so, everything is fucked up but I don't think we owe anybody anything, so if you want to take over this leaking laughing boat, fine. I'll presume that you will and I will forward all *Laugh Lit*. mail to you, o.k.? although lately I have been telling the submitters that *Laugh* is dead so they prob. will not come around again. no loss, from what I read.

ah, Steve, the FEMALE. there is no way. don't wait for the good woman. she doesn't exist. there are women who can make you feel more with their bodies and their souls but these are the exact women who will turn the knife into you right in front of the crowd. of course, I expect this, but the knife still cuts. the female loves to play man against man. and if she is in a position to do it there is not one who will not resist. the male, for all his bravado and exploration, is the loyal one, the one who generally feels love. the female is skilled at betrayal. and torture and damnation. never envy a man his lady. behind it all lays a living hell. I know you're not going to quit the chase, but when you go into it, for Christ's sake, realize that you are going to be burned ahead of time. never go in totally *open*. the madhouses and skidrows are full of those. remember, the female is any man's woman at any time. the choice is hers. and she's going to rip the son of a bitch she goes to just like she ripped you. but never hate the woman. understand that she is channeled this way and let her go. solitude too brings a love as tall as the mountains. fuck the skies. amen.

god, I talk more about cunt than I do about literature. literature is a hairy cunt. I know how to love a woman but a good poem will last longer, and almost every man can have a hairy cunt. put your chips on a winner – on the inner-gut sight. if you treat it well it will never betray you. and

laugh literary and MAN THE HUMPING GUNS, baby.

[To John Martin]
November 19, 1971

Thanks for sending the Wakoski books. I should get into them soon. I know that she has a nice loose line that does not restrict her thinking like most of those slick-ass men.

I am still going through a certain phrasology (spell?) that is taking some of the energy from my writing, but it's explorative, and, I think, hardly life-taking – say, as the Post Office was. I think, in the end (if I last) it will pay off in the writing, not only now but later, and it will also pay off as a chunk of real-ass living. Of course, I'm making a lot of errors. I always have. It's almost that by going wrong I get to the mother light. I think you know what I mean.

I just turned down two offers to drink tonight – their booze – too many good-time Charlies like to suck off of my energy. All right, like I say, after the Jon Webb[1] memoriam thing, we walk back into the buzzsaw of the poetry-prose blaze, and HOW IS OUR NEW BOOK OF POEMS COMING ALONG, DEAR FATHER? I need a new book of poems . . . it has been quite some time. get to work on it, get to work, get to work, get to work, on it . . . [★ ★ ★]

[To Gregory Maronick]
November 26, 1971

Thanks for the letter. I think that if some of your students hate me, it's a good sign. I think if they all hated me it would be a better sign. If I ever get as loved as Rod McKuen I'll know I'm as bad as R.M. What defines a poetry as poetry or any art form as an art form is puzzling. I suppose it takes a century or so and then, even then, I feel we're often mistaken. All a man can do is write what he feels like writing. This isn't as easy as it sounds; to get down to yourself takes all manner of things, but bad luck, madness, such things help. Don't let me preach. All right. I won't.

I ran out of the post office to a typewriter to try my luck. At first, it was all right. Readings, stories in sex mags; poems on the side. Then along came the tight money situation. The readings stopped. The sex mags, which used to pay 30 days after acceptance, have not only halved their rates but I now have 2 or 3 stories on the stands and I haven't even received the purchase orders yet. On top of this I have met this mad woman 20 years younger than myself. She is a tremendous flirt, hits on men continually, dances like a hot whore, but she doesn't fuck the guys, but it's such a drag, and she's nice in bed and when she's nice she's nice out of bed, but she's schitzi, has done time, and she has these tremendous runs of ups and downs, plus and minus. I get down plenty myself. I can

---

1. Jon Webb had died on June 9, 1971.

look the other way on a lot of things except maybe just simple rudeness and unfeelingness. I don't mean to slop all this over you. But it's been one god damned battle after another. This eats into creative time. This eats into everything. We split 2 or 3 times a week. Simple madness. But it's destructive and I'm trying to work my way out of it. Like yesterday, I lay out 15 bucks and here's this big turkey on the table and all the other stuff, her two kids have eaten, my kid has eaten, next thing I know we're at each other and I'm walking out the door. She phones collect at my place 3 hours later, pretending she is another lady (?), but it's her and she claims she's in Phoenix. Goodbye, I say, and hang up. I mean, this goes on and on. It eats. If she found another guy or I found a kinder woman, we could both let go. It's killing. I don't mean to be unfair but I do think she came by because she had read my books, some of them anyhow, and she thought it might be interesting to see what this writer was. That's no way to move in on a man. She sees me sitting in a chair, she doesn't see me, she sees a Charles Bukowski. I can't perform Charles Bukowski for her, I am sick of that son of a bitch. I swear, if I ever meet a *kind* woman I don't care if she has a wooden leg or a glass eye or both or all, I'll run off to Alaska with her or China or East Lansing and we'll live together and die together. By kind, I don't mean a woman who will kiss my ass, I mean a woman who is simply gentle by nature. All these L.A. women are HARD. Their eyes are hard, their movements, their calculations. Maybe they have to be. maybe I'm hard too. I don't think so. My poems, maybe, but me, no. ah ah ah. [★ ★ ★]

Big crazy kid over last night. We got to talking about PAIN, about the world out there and about going on, how hard it was just to go on, you know, the way the women were, the way everything was. And I told the kid, "Listen, you know how it happens. Sometimes I'm in the bedroom, just kind of walking around, like I'm looking for a paperclip, and it hits me – PAIN – it's like a guy has punched me in the stomach – I double over and hold my stomach – I can feel the spot – I can feel the HOLE – it's pain, the terror, the not understanding – I've had ulcers, that's not it – this is just the thing coming down and getting you . . ." "I know," he said, "I get the same thing. Sometimes I cry. It's a silent crying but I can feel the tears running down . . ."

So, you see, Gregory, the way isn't easy for any of us. Dylan drank his way out. Hem and Van Gogh liked shotguns. Chatterton rat poison. I can feel it now as I am typing. I am saying to the sounds of the typewriter, make it go away, make everything go away, but it doesn't. I can see it out there now. DeLongpre Ave. The world. A spiderweb of dung. Survival is an indecent dribbling spittle. o.k.

[To John Martin]
December 3, 1971

Gertrude Stein, eh? Who's that? While all us young writers starve . . . God, it's dark. It rained last night. I got out of a warm bed in Burbank and drove home in the rain and when I got there the wind Gertrude Steined through the broken glass of my front door and I sat there shivering and drinking my tiny bottle of Schlitz wondering when the elephants were going to come along and kick some decent shit literature out of me, and meanwhile, here's the enclosed.

• 1972 •

John Berryman committed suicide on January 7, 1972 and Kenneth Patchen died on January 8.

[To Carl Weissner]
January [?10], 1972

[* * *] well, Patchen left and John Berryman jumped off a bridge last Friday and they haven't found him yet. They say Berryman was on a quart of whiskey a day, or so somebody told me. I never saw him or it. The field narrows, babe, and there doesn't seem to be anything else coming on.

I heard from one of your buddies, Joris, in London. He's on some kind of onion, trying to translate me into the French. Another guy I know is fumbling me into Italian. Also, some guy teaching French at U.C.L.A. is working on getting some poems of mine into the French, so, shit, it's buzzing . . . Recession here, and mags like *Knight, Adam*, have more than halved their rates . . . which means I gotta write twice as many dirty stories. This writing game is more desperate than holding up liquor stores, yet I'm snared in now and there's no out. A man's ass finally gets lazy, too lazy and the mind gets too crazy to do any damned job. Now I'm almost too lazy to write. An empty belly and rent due, might stove that up a bit, though. Norse pulled out of Venice and went weeping up to S.F. in search of kinder souls . . . I'm still on with the sculptress and it's unsolvable . . . I judge everything – women, no women, booze, no booze – on my writing. I'm writing better but less. There, that's sensible. [* * *]

[To John Martin] [from Phoenix, Arizona]
January 12, 1972

Well, I'm out in the desert and I can use the check. Mother, it's hot in here, they turn the heat too high . . . well, tomorrow I'm going to try to set up in the cacti somewhere with this machine and get into some poems, stories, the novel . . . I've been lax long enough. There are 4 or 5 sisters and a friend out here; they're all writing novels . . . every place you turn you see another writer. blind guy came in – he's writing two novels. writers, writers, writers – I leave DeLongpre to get rid of that gang and here I am surrounded again. Well, there may be a story in all this; meanwhile I'm with Linda, which is fulfilling when we're on. gangs of children running through, dogs, relatives, tv going, but it's all fairly nice – they tend to ignore me which is a good way of being accepted. [* * *]

[To John Martin]
January 17, 1972

[* * *] I don't understand this desert out here. It looks like something that wanted to give up but didn't know quite how. The brush is yellow, no, brown and tired and desperate. And the horses and cattle, they just don't care. They lay or stand and wait, wait, wait, Everything here is waiting. That's the feel of it. Or like this is the last edge of the world and it's all too tired to fall off. The cowboys, too, seem indifferent. The people. They walk around and their faces show neither pain or concern or worry. They are like their horses and cattle. Well, that's good and a change from L.A.-Hollywood where everybody is hard and on the hustle and with the front, and most of them not having it at all. Well, hell.

[* * *] There are 3 typewriters going at once here. Can I have set these sisters on fire? Hello to Barbara. Bukowski marches on. He'll live to be 80. I always wanted to die in the year 2,000. Of course, the whole gang of us may leave at once before then, or almost at once. A cat below where I am typing just grabbed my toe, bit and scratched it. There's something cooking in the kitchen; the love is good, the cat climbs my leg now, purring and digging in his "fingernails," as Linda's daughter calls them . . . Is this the literary life? Why not? The fire from the devil's beard stews the afternoon air. Don't give up on me. uh uh.

[To Carl Weissner]
January [?18], 1972

well, god damn, here I am in Phoenix, Ariz. [* * *] and I ought to be here until Feb. 10 or 12th this year, if I don't go giraffe . . . like one time I was out here and couldn't bear up under conditions and I took me a 3 hour stroll in the desert. It seems easier this time — so far. staying here with my gal friend and her sister, and there's another sister on another ranch across the way, and I play the poet-writer but so far as writing goes I've done little, have made local racetrack — Turf Paradise — 3 times with moderate success driving my gal's polka dot car with Calif. license plates, and I now got me kinda long hair and a shitty beard and there is madness in my eyes, of course, and I like driving around in the polka dot, the locals don't get the angle — there isn't any.

by the way, you see Herman, you tell him I ain't pissed because my girlfriend kissed him goodbye when he came over to see me. I made her kiss 5 guys at the end of one of my parties to show them what they're missing; of course, I frown upon anybody else fucking her — I tend to like the unmolested pisshole. [* * *]

these 3 sisters are all mad, sexy, intelligent, liberal . . . and they're all writing novels . . . about sex, oral copulation, insanity . . . and the cactus is out there, and there's beer and smokes and change and evenings when you can see the bored stars, I stand, old companion, with you in the battle, we will have both victory and death, fire and water, love and hate, noon and midnight, I wish you plenty, well, hang in.

[To Carl Weissner]
February [?5], 1972

got your damn good letter, it was a laugher.

meanwhile, one of the sisters got down on me because I didn't accept her writing or her as a mighty good thing and she screamed and screamed, many things, like, "my children are my novels," and so forth, then she railed against my writing. I got on out. she's 41, never been published. well, that's all right; but even if she were published I'd still think she was a bad writer. well, so I left early. back here. Linda looking for a place — 2 children and a dog. not easy. we are jammed in here.

can't walk around. no way to write. well, man, it's all for the good of the fire.[★ ★ ★]

I'll try to get the City Lights book to you when it comes out. I do think the stories fouler (better) than *Notes of a D. O. Man*. Instead of calling it Bukowskiana (not my idea), I have retitled it *Erections, Ejaculations, Exhibitions and General Tales of Ordinary Madness*. At the printer's now, says L.F. He calls it a great book. I agree. I don't think that since Artaud or Nietzsche there has been anybody as joyfully mad as I am. well.

well, this is just to let you know the bare things & that I am alive and your letters are always a pleasure, works of Art, my friend, and yes, I know how it must be with the ladies, we must give them all the extras of tongue and touch, because that's a creation too, making a lady truly hot, and, at the same time we must get away from them long enough to create . . . I think the man who said, The strongest men are the most alone, was right.[1] I suppose I will have to get back to that. Even though I believe I love Linda. We tear ourselves apart for the typewriter, for those one or 2 lines. and it's worth it . . .

The book being referred to in the following is Mockingbird, Wish Me Luck, *published June 1972.*

[To John Martin]
February 6, 1972

[★ ★ ★] I've done ten of the drawings for our book of poems. I don't say much about it but each time a book comes out I get just as excited as the first time. I don't suppose this is very professional, but isn't this what it's about? I mean, a book, a tabulation? it makes it much easier to die, somehow, except you don't want to die because you want to do more. getting published in the magazines doesn't raise up much in me, but a book is holy [*sic*] another matter. I have a feeling that this book of poems

---

1. Perhaps "The strongest man is he who stands alone," Halldor Laxness, *Independent People* (trans. 1945), quoted by Brad Leithauser, *New York Review of Books*, May 11, 1995, p. 44. But see the letter of November 15, 1974, below, where Bukowski attributes the remark to Ibsen.

will be the best. I warm up all through the arms and chest and belly thinking about it.

[* * *] this is a difficult life – because I am more open to things that happen – but compared to the Post Office and the hundred other jobs, it's life lighting up near the end, and it's worth it all – the gamble, the doubt; at least when I get my lazy ass up and at it, my energy is going where my feelings are, and there's no way of short-selling a value like that. Cheer up, Sparrow. [* * *]

A. D. Winans edited Second Coming *magazine from 1972 onward.*

[To A. D. Winans]
February 16, 1972

Yes, thanks for copy of *Second Coming*. I had a second coming myself the other night, which is fairly fair for my age. Re: your *Second Coming*, I thought the content all right but too much emphasis on prose. I like a balance between prose and poetry, *plus* one or 2 very nasty reviews of life, books or anything. As much as we look down on the academy, I always remember the old days, coming off the park benches and into the libraries and reading those very phoney yet bitchingly beautiful reviews in the old *Kenyon Review*. But never mind all that. [* * *]

An Anthology of L.A. Poets, *edited by Bukowski, Neeli Cherry, and Paul Vangelisti, was published by* Laugh Literary *in 1972.*

[To John Martin]
March 14, 1972

[* * *] Neeli, Paul and I are going to put out *An Anthology of L.A. Poets*. I think it has long been needed. This town has been smeared long enough both as a place to live and a place to create. Of course, it *does* have Hollywood attached to it but L.A. needn't be a Siamese twin. Many people live here and ignore Hollywood, Disneyland and the L.A. Dodgers completely and also Alvera street and Broadway and

Hill and the Rose Parade and the Santa Claus Parade. L.A. is really still the Grand Central Market and Alvarado st. and Main st. and E. 5th and E. L.A. Watts is fairly Hollywood. Watts has been tricked. But may bounce back. [★ ★ ★]

[To John Martin]
March 31, 1972

[★ ★ ★] Regarding your phone call, I have some down moments but I don't think I'm about to go just yet, especially if I stay away from the whiskey. You know, the writing must come out of the living, the reaction to living. If I get a little scorched now and then, it's all for the good of the barbecue. And when the leisure time is needed in order to get it down, that time is there and I think it makes the writing solider. Forgive me if it doesn't.

On Linda, it has to end sooner or later. In 9 more years she'll be 40 years old. I just can't tolerate them thar old women, dude. [★ ★ ★]

[To Carl Weissner]
June [?20], 1972

[★ ★ ★] The sculptress and I split. She went back to her hometown in Utah. But there seem to be a great many long distance calls and letters going back and forth between us. I didn't wait long. I jumped right into bed with a 43 years old gal who is president of some record company. My personality isn't very good but I throw good fucks for a 52 year old guy. "You just couldn't wait," says the sculptress, "you just had to go jump into bed!" "But, baby, I thought . . ."

The new one is very kind and says she loves me but it just doesn't seem the same as the other one, it just ain't, and I don't know what the hell. The sculptress phoned and I was going up to Utah and then the new one heard and swallowed a handful of sleeping pills. I stuck my fingers down her throat and made her vomit, and called the trip off. I am caught in between all this. And there's no solving it, it will never be solved. [★ ★ ★]

remember when you came to the U.S. and I couldn't pick you up at the airport? I became stricken? airports and space were beyond me, I hope you understand. since then I've flown a dozen times and I bounce in and out of space ports like a human flea. too bad I wasn't ready for you. I grow so slowly. Sorry.

I truly don't understand the ladies, Carl. They seem to exert terrific pressures while asking a kind of freedom of their own. I am puzzled beyond puzzlement. Any clues? My problem is that I seem to care too much. How the hell can I get out of that?

[To Lafayette Young]
June 25, 1972

Thanks plenty for the clothes for Marina. I'm going to see her the monday from next and you just don't know how happy she'll be with them. She doesn't have much to wear, I suppose I should do better, but anyhow the clothes and purses, all that great stuff will be put to a mighty use: to make a beautiful little girl more beautiful. thank you, friend.

the human race? god jesus, save us from it, somehow. I hang in and wait to die. just got off a bad experience – 16 months – with a woman. trying to put myself together again. I'm now with another. it's gentler but hardly as stimulating. well, it's a day at a time, and it has never been easy.

hang in.

William J. Robson edited and published Holy Doors: an Anthology of Poetry, Prose, and Criticism *from Long Beach, California (1972). He had previously, in 1970, published* Looking for the Giants: an interview with Charles Bukowski.

[To Bill Robson]
July 11, 1972

Now that Richmond and Fox have me down as failing, a liar, a sell-out, so forth, it's curious that you still want to hear from me. Don't you believe them? Don't you realize that I am a ruined man? That I have forsaken the truth, all that shit? I don't know how to answer these boys.

They both seem to be staking a claim as real writers, overlooked, for this reason or that. Whatever the grounds of their bitching wails, I only ask that you measure the totality of all my work against theirs and make a judgment.

Poor Fox. He claims Black Sparrow published me because I was "known" and didn't publish him because he was "unknown." He claims the quality of his work had nothing to do with it. I have no idea of John Martin's worded rejection of the Fox manuscript. It was probably kindly-worded and Fox read into it what he wanted to read into it. The real fact was that the poetry probably was simply bad stuff.

This bit about the "known" and the "unknown" is ridiculous. No writer is born "known." They don't know us in our cradle, or in our rompers or in our schoolyards. We have to become "known." And if a writer remains "unknown" long enough there's usually a good reason for it.

Fox and Richmond seem to think I have "sold out" because I make my living with my typewriter. I have even labeled myself "a literary hustler," but where is their sense of humor? The story in *Rogue* was not crap or some cheap little bullshit formula story for a buck, as Fox might say. He might read the story again. He likens me to the prof in *Blue Angel*, egg broken over head ... Christ, these little snippets, these tiny little quarter talents ... they really want to do me in ... They know that my work is better than ever and that I am getting *paid* for it, and that's their attack — I make the money writing: therefore the writing must be a sell-out.

Fox from his professional post advises writers to go get a job and write on the side. I've had a hundred jobs and I wrote on the side. I worked until I was 50 in the most slave-labor and demeaning jobs imaginable. That doesn't create literature; it only tires your ass out. Fox chirps to his students and Richmond lays in the sun outside his beach cottage, claiming to be worth only $300. All I say is that the real ARENA is CREATION. Let them get into that arena instead of bitching like neurotic housewives over the backyard fence. I'm afraid that the small presses, the mimeo presses have kept alive too many talentless darlings, and have made life difficult for their wives, their children, their girlfriends.

I don't believe that in getting paid for what you do, that being a professional, necessarily detracts from your art. It may detract from yours, it doesn't from mine. Many people get paid for what they do. And they do all right. Starvation and obscurity are not necessarily signs of genius.

Let Time itself answer the attacks on me by Richmond and Fox. As for me, I've wasted enough time on them. Oh, my little friends, how you cry and weep and bawl and puke and slobber over yourselves. May I suggest that you use more of your energy on what you pretend is your craft – that is: writing. There seems room for improvement. Some day you may be men.

[To Patricia Connell]
July 31, 1972

Hello Patricia Connell:

Thanks for your letter. Very interesting stationery. Too bad you didn't come along with it. It's not every day that this dirty old man hears from an airline stewardess – though most of them piss me off for one reason or another when I ride them, or rather, their plane. I suppose it's because they're all so god damned casual. If only one of them would break a leg some day or drop a uterus. Still, I suppose somebody *does* read my column and/or my books. I'm largely underground with a red nose from drinking beer and I'll be 52 in August, the 16th. That doesn't leave much left over. I just broke off with a 31 year old girl, a looker, 16 mad screaming months, and I've told Liza not to love me. There. Tah tah taha.

If your pilots tend to go my stuff, there's a large jumbo collection of my stories just out, *Erections, Ejaculations, Exhibitions and General Tales of Ordinary Madness*. It goes for $3.95 via City Lights. [★ ★ ★]

[To Patricia Connell]
August 3, 1972

So you're 27 years old! I'm just mad about young women, they drive me ape, completely out of context and/or reality, but I don't give a damn. Don't know if I've mentioned but I just got over a 16 month affair with a 31 year old sculptress. We fucked and sucked and loved and slept together, ate breakfast together, lunch together, everything together – fighting, mortally wounded, she was a Carmen, that one, beautiful and cruel, a flirt, a vamp, a woman, a most wondrous woman. She finally ran off to Utah when I walked out on her once too often. With Liza I'm honest, I tell her, don't love me, please don't love me . . .

I'd like to come see you – you haven't invited me – but my dear old 62 Comet needs a bit of repair work . . . Manhattan Beach? – that's where my wife split when she divorced me – she was a millionairess – I married her through the mail – sight unseen – when she kept writing that no man would ever marry her – there was something wrong with her neck – she couldn't turn her neck – I said, kid, I got scars all over me, I look like a punchboard, I'll marry you – she was all right, for a while, until she knew I didn't love her. Manhattan Beach. That's it. Yes.

I hesitate to phone. Phone conversations are difficult. Just think how we'd look together? I could pose as your father. Until we got to bed. I do all right in bed. Not that I'm exceptionally hung but I go down on that thing with some artistry and believe in the long ride. . . . Is this what you'd call shooting the shit? I know that most men who claim to be great lovers are nothing but on and off jackrabbits. Listen, how did we get into all this sex bit?

I worked most of my life on dull labor jobs but 2 years ago quit and layed it all on the typewriter. I'm not getting rich but I'm still alive. 7 year old daughter in Santa Monica. I volunteer 45 bucks a month child support. I like lobster, beer, and occasional racetrack (computer data?), young women, especially those around 27 with a job dishing out those two drinks in the sky. I am emotional and kind and ride around in a big tank so people won't stick pins into me. The sculptress said, I don't think I ever met a guy with a line like yours. And Liza says, "I never met a man who made better love." So there you have it, plus and minus. I don't think I have a line. Well.

I don't expect you to like all my writing – prose or poetry. No matter what you do, some people are going to like it, some are going to dislike it, and the vast majority aren't going to give a damn one way or the other. [★ ★ ★]

The man-woman relationship is fraught with pain and glory and warmth and wonderment. It's certainly worth the trip. I've liked your letters, they show insight. I'd like to see you some time. For all my talk, I'm very slow. I don't like to rush. I don't want to get into anything that I don't want to stay in for some time. I'm sentimental as all shit. It's my nature. I'm tough too. I can be a son of a birch when I have to be and sometimes I have to be.

Save these letters. They're worth money. You may need money some day, dear, when people stop flying United and fly angels. I'm really not a male chauv. pig. Be good, Patricia.

Bukowski (fly me!)

[To Patricia Connell]
August 8, 1972

You're right – there's a lot of self-destruct in my relationships . . . The sculptress and I practically lived together – but there seemed two violent whirling flaming battles a week – break-up, make-up – it was vibrant enough and the love was great and the sex was great, and when it was all going well you couldn't beat it – but . . . Now with Liza there are hardly any arguments, it's all very smooth, but, at least from my viewpoint, it's not the grand flame . . . so I asked her not to love me. The sculptress was coming back to me from Utah once or twice and Liza acted up quite badly – I won't go into details but it was a mess, and I don't want to see her get that way again. Oh, I'm capable of love, my child, I've been in love twice in 52 years. I didn't love the sculptress but now I realize that something in our personalities will never leave us at peace. so I had to tell her that I had given up on our relationship. That's the package.

Oh, I'm Buk, not Buck. Pronounced Buke.

Ah, the seriousness of old age, you say. Well, I don't know. A certain lady says that no man has made love to her like I do. I'm the best of the bloody lot, and she's known hundreds. I can't help taking some pride in that statement. I intend to live until 80 and to ball until 80 and to go down until 80, and if this seems crude, so be it.

It was good talking to you on the phone. I liked your voice and you had an easy manner, you made me feel comfortable.

Yes, I'd like to have a beer with you some time. We needn't make a large thing of it. I don't believe in trapping people or chasing them down, or vice versa. Also, there's no rush, although I have to leave town in Sept. a couple of times for poetry readings – one for Ferlinghetti at S.F. and one at the Univ. of Arizona. Meanwhile my poor car is getting a blood transfusion. Somehow it feels good to hear from you and to rather be in touch. I hope to hear something from you, and to eventually set up our famous meeting over a beer . . . Size? I'm 5' 11" and ¾'s, 210 pounds. I'm Leo. Like beer, boxing matches, horse races; like to drive women crazy on the lovebed. Or so says the computer. I'll always try to fly United, so help me, little one. I'm influenced by Celine, Dostoevski, Kafka, classical music, myself, the miracle of the female and the general weathers of life. Hell, write me when the mood moves ye.

[To Patricia Connell]
August 11, 1972

Oh, *Post Office*. I wrote that in twenty drunken nights on scotch and cigars. Don't expect too much.

I phoned the sculptress last night on a lark. She's moving back to town in Sept. "I'm not coming to you, Bukowski. I'm going to think of all the evil things you did to me. A week before I come back I'm going to get some guy to fuck me for a week so I won't need you."

Well, the female is a clever creature. She knows how to regulate her affairs. Most often it is the man who falls apart; it's the man who jumps off the bridge. When we give over our feelings they run off with us. There's no regulating them. I give over my feelings too easily, and it's not all relegated to suck and fuck (as the sculptress calls it). I get as much, or more, out of the other parts. Small talk. Breakfast together. Sleeping while touching. Waiting while the other goes to the toilet. Love-making after a stupid argument. Drinking beer with maddened friends. Hundreds of tiny things. I am never bored when I am with my woman. I get bored in large formless crowds. Bored, hell, I get desperate, I lather and blather at the mouth, my eyes roll, the sky shakes. What am I talking about here?

And you're strange. Why do you want to meet a 52 year old man? (I'll be 52 this August 16th. Wish me a happy birthday.) Is your father dead? Or didn't you have much of a father? If we like each other somewhat I can be your father, but on the other hand, I'm very horny. Was your father very horny?

My guess is that you've gotten too much attention and found it wanting – jackrabbits, fly-by-nights, so forth. Young men are too stricken with themselves to be human. I can stand by you while you wait for the arrival of the proper one. My god, we're getting serious here, aren't we? Uggg. Well, it's hot, the weather's hot and I went to the boxing matches last night and spilled beer on myself. Then over to Liza's. I must be careful not to hurt Liza. She's a kind and a good woman but I don't love her.

Anyhow, the boxing matches were good. Everybody screamed. Even the fighters enjoyed it. And there you go flying to Richmond, Virginia. I think we should meet but I don't want you to meet a stranger – hence the letters, a bit of talking. I find myself thinking about you at odd moments during the day and I don't even know who you are – flying out there over Richmond – all those oilmen dandies and insurance dandies, all with that satisfied look, twisting the rocks in their scotch as the satisfied pilot gargles some inanity over the intercom, yes, yes, perhaps we can meet and perhaps we can hate each other right off, get it done with, clean the deck and look for the next pink cloud, what? But your letters have been warm, and I have the feeling that you've been through some things and come out better for them. Keep in touch, Pattie, you make the mailbox look good.

[To Patricia Connell]
August 16, 1972 [52nd birthday]

'tis very stimulating to get a letter from a woman, and a very young one at that. I got in about ten thirty and there was your letter, very fat, warm like a glove, the bit on the back, this girl looking inside this man's head and kind of playing with him spiritually. ah. there was some other mail and I read it first, then got a beer and opened yours. there had been a postcard from England, "have just finished your city lights book and have found it the best writing of short stories since Cervantes and Dickens and Walter Scott . . ." now, uh huh, that's high praise, as they call it. for dirty stories, that's o.k. anyhow, I went through your letter to try to find out who you were, and if you're a little sarcastic, that's o.k. I like being insulted, it charms me. that's what got me going with the sculptress, she was sitting there doing my head and she looked at me and said, "My husband said when I divorced him that he hoped I would meet a real crud, and now I have." I laughed. it was too delightful. I've got to have this woman, I thought, even if she's only 30, I've got to have her. well, we lasted 16 months, but looking back now I see it was mostly sex and battle. we went 4 or 5 times a week, right on through periods and all and fought and split forever twice a week. it was total flame and madness and it finally broke wide open. I phoned her last night and finally ended up hanging up on her. there's no getting together. all our ideas seem opposite. she said before she moves back to town she's going to fuck some guy for a week so she won't need me. And, to me, that was the tipoff – I am just a sex machine for her servicing. to hell with that. I've got nothing against sex, I'm all for it; there's nothing I like better than to really satisfy a woman. It's an art and I like to be a good artist. But I also like to feel some warmth outside the sexual relationship.

I think we should meet. I am not a pushy person. And I'm *very* EASY to get rid of. Liza calls me a bashful madman. Maybe I am. We should get a few drinks between us when we meet . . . easing of tension, you know. it's really a very difficult thing. you are a stranger to me. you *know* something about me because you've read some of my shit. Can we meet during a day sometime? Frankly, I'm over at Liza's each night, and I don't want to hurt her. She's in love with me, for one reason or another she's in love with me, and she knows I don't love her, yet still I don't want to hurt her. We had one or two split scenes where she almost cracked – the suicide bit, you know and I've been on the love-end and I've been hurt by the other, and the pain is intolerable, unbelievable, so I want to be careful with Liza, yet since I don't love her I still feel I have a right to see some other women. does this sound like bullshit? well, it's not.

I'll be in Frisco Sept. 14 giving a reading and at the Univ. of Arizona Sept. 28, reading, and outside of that my time is my own. But that's Sept. this is August and I'm 52 years old writing a half a love letter to a 27 year old airline stewardess, o, the world is mad, isn't it? but great too. can you tell me when a good day would be? Sat and Sunday, I think, would be bad days. can you draw me a map, how to get there? my car's running but best to stay off freeways. no auto insurance. do you believe in sex, or do you just want a talking relationship, or what? or do you want to see what happens? let it flow? tell me things. I'm selfish, you know. I think a sex-love relationship with you would produce a great many poems, love poems. the whole last third of my last poem book, *Mockingbird*, are love poems to Linda. you see all I want you for? just for my typewriter, Pattie Connell, just for the ticking of the keys. . . .

I think it's good for a woman to meet a great many men, in bed and out of bed, so that when the good man comes along she'll know why.

I enjoyed your long letter, even though you seem a little evasive. Is the man you're going with very jealous? Do you love him? Does he go down on you? Does he do it right? I mean, are you getting anything out of it? or are you just going through some rote thing for lack of anything else to do? you know, many men are satisfied with their women because they satisfy themselves upon them, but few men really satisfy their women.

they're simply too selfish. that's why I didn't mind Linda being 30, because I took proper care of her.

I celebrated my birthday a bit early yesterday. A lawyer dropped by, and then Liza, and we had a few drinks. A few too many. "Look," I said, "here I'm sitting with a corporate lawyer and a record executive, and I'm a starving poet. What the hell are you people doing here?"

I haven't been to the racetrack in some weeks. Del Mar is such a long haul . . . Linda is going with a homosexual now. I told her it was a cop-out. that she should get a real man and face the fire and the glory.

All right, Pattie, I think we should have a meeting. nothing oppressive or up-tight, maybe a little nervous, but with nobody owing anybody anything. loose, you know. you might hate me on sight. I'm hardly pretty and hardly a normal type human being. In fact, I'm pretty badly fucked up. Crazed, Liza calls it. but I'm hardly dangerous or maniacal or any of that shit. I suppose you'd call me a kind person. well, my god. some out of work actor just called up and wished me a happy birthday. he's stuck in some factory, working the swing shift. we're all trying to make it, this way or that, trying to find love, trying to find sex, trying to find peace and meaning before we hang it up. I look at these 52 years gone by and I know now that I don't know any more than I did at 18. That's not much growth, is it? ah, let me hear from you on all matters. I'm sentimental and I get attached to women but I wouldn't force anything on you. I have an idea I couldn't. you must be fairly sophisticated, running up and down those aisles, jostling and chatting with the passengers, getting pinched by the pilots. I'm more raw and clumsy. maybe you can teach me some polish. when I get up to read my poems I sound like one of those old fashioned victrolas, running down. but you wouldn't know about them. there are no bluebirds in my skies, Patricia, and the sun blinks on and off. looks like rain. last night I had all these rain dreams. it kept raining and raining and raining. do you think I'm out of my craw? christ, well, write me, little one. I think all this is quite wonderful.

some kind of love, Buk.

[To Carl Weissner]
August 16, 1972

[★ ★ ★] I just got rid of a bad one, and once again I seem to be making moves toward 2 young girls. one is 27, the other I think is 20. I shouldn't. I must be going crazy. the one I'm with, she's 43, treats me gently. gave me $70 for my birthday the other day. Needed tires for my car, various parts. a good woman. but I'm so used to bad women, whores, flirts, vamps, sluts, liars, madwomen. when I grow up I am going to break off from all of them. that's the system, that's the out. [★ ★ ★]

[To Patricia Connell]
August 18, 1972

Thanks for the birthday card, 'twas touching. You're still on *Post Office*, I suppose. You should read *Erections* . . . via City Lights, a better work. Either/Or [bookshop] should have had it. I haven't read Kosinski but he was put on me. A gal came by one time, she used to dance with a ten foot boa constrictor on the Sunset strip – she's in Berkeley now – and she put the book onto me but I passed it on without reading. The boa constrictor lady was ready for consummation at the moment, and still is, but I wasn't ready.

I'm supposed to go to Del Mar this Weds. or Thursday. With Liza and a couple of guys from a tv station. they want to put me on an education television thing. They seem serious but last time I saw them we all just got drunk. It's supposed to go on 65 tv stations across the nation but so far there hasn't been a click of video tape or whatever. such non-going shit can last into eternity.

So you're a sadist, eh? God, the sculptress was a cruel woman too. It seems quite standard, doesn't it? I suppose men beg too much and this gives the ladies this feeling of power. You've got all these little men on your shelf. O.k. When you gonna put me on your shelf?

I really should do some work with this typer today, but wanted to thank you for the card. Write when you feel free to do so.

[To Patricia Connell]
August 21, 1972

It's noon, slight hangover, coffee on, going to Santa Monica soon to see my daughter – she's 7.

Yes, I suppose we should meet. I lay claim to being the world's ugliest man. Perhaps we can meet, hate each other right off and get it done with.

A relationship without love is comfortable because you are always in control if the other person loves you. But the one who is in love really has the benefits because (he) (she) is thriving, throbbing, vibrating. I would certainly rather be in love if I had a choice but one doesn't always have this choice. I've only been in love twice in 52 years.

For a person who is supposedly afraid of people you are very open with me. And it would take guts to meet me. It would not be an easy thing. I don't think you have too much fear of people.

I've been going with Liza since May 2nd when Linda and I split. I jumped right out of one bed and into another. I suppose that makes me a bastard. I don't like to sleep alone.

We could have a friendship. Or let it start that way if it wanted to. Sex is damned nice but not necessary. A Thursday evening might be nice. But I won't want to drink too much because I have to drive back and already have one drunk driving rap. Liza goes out and has drinks and dinner with these 2 guys every Thursday night. Yes, I have a nightly vigil by Liza's side as you say. But there aren't any chains on me. I just don't want to mess her up. If you and I ever got anything going she would have to fall by the way. But it seems senseless to hurt her without that. She's a record company exec. and plenty of men are after her. I'm rather honored that she preferred me to all the young handsome men but she'll hardly be alone if we ever split.

A little luck in the mail today. A German publisher wants to translate *Erections, Ejaculations, Exhibitions and General Tales of Ordinary Madness* into the Hun. But we're waiting on Rowolt – the largest German publisher – and if they go it I won't be driving that 62 Comet much longer.

I enjoy your letters very much. Get relaxing with that Bloody Mary soon and tell me some more things.

[To Carl Weissner]
August [?30], 1972

[★ ★ ★] The sculptress is back. Saw her yesterday. "Listen," she said, "you're in a triangle now. You're trying to hold 2 women at once. It can't be done."

"They do it in the movies sometimes," I said.

Anyhow, we got into an argument and I cut out of there. her face looked strangely hard after that 4 month's separation, and her eyes too. I'm afraid something has gone out of it for me. I don't love the other one either. Krist, I'm not in a triangle at all. I'm nowhere. the female is a monumental puzzle to me. I must be strong enough to do without them, without her and her and her. A lot of dirty laundry and haggling. [★ ★ ★]

[To Patricia Connell]
September 13, 1972

I've been into a lot of shit and so I'm late in getting this off to you. Up to Frisco tomorrow – PSA – Hollywood – Burbank to give a reading. They claim it's the largest SF crowd since Yevtushenko the Russian poet. The auditorium holds 750 and they claim to be sold out. I hope they are. I get half the god damned take and at 2 bucks a head maybe I can afford a cold beer when I get back. 750 for Billy Graham ain't cat's turds but for poetry it's something. o, yeh, I write poems too, kitten.

A fine photo thanks. Youze is a lovely lovely thing. I gotta meet ya some day if only to look at ya. I mean, look, I wrote you all these letters. That's work.

I broke off with Liza and went back to the sculptress (Linda). Liza took it hard. She read me off good. I talked to her for 7 hours about it, during which time she beat the shit out of me 5 times. I let her beat on me because I felt bad about what I was doing to her. But she'll make it. She has a good job and plenty of men are after her, or her money. She's really a fine person and should never have put her trust in a slob like me, but the sculptress has this immense pull on me, I am helpless. She just walks in and I'm finished. I don't have any excuses except that I might love the sculpt. and I didn't love Liza.

All that sounds like vomit in the beef stew, doesn't it? A mess. Well.

Anyhow, I'm not much good at triangles so I had to pull out from one or the other.

You sound like you're getting love-security from a man you want and don't want. I'd rather imagine you're shopping around for the spark, that's why you're dating other men. If your man doesn't walk out on you it may be more from weakness than strength. Or maybe I'm wrong.

I've got to line up the poems for the reading, so this will be fairly short. – I enjoyed your telling of the Tom Jones bit. Those jackasses get *so* spoiled.

We ought to meet some day when the climate is right for both of us. Easy does it, you know.

You exclaimed that my letters were too short when I phoned you. Listen, kitten, if I wrote mine in longhand like yours they'd look pretty long, you know. Ah, our FIRST ARGUMENT!!! Isn't it great?

[To Patricia Connell]
September 18, 1972

ah, I am back with Liza. Went north with Linda for the reading, came back all scratched up. I broke if off with Linda on grounds I'd rather not go into. anyhow, she threatened to kill me. Liza has also threatened to kill me. interesting life, what? Linda's schitzy and when she's up or right I love her very much but when she shows the other side, it's too much. Liza is really a fine woman, though I don't love her. channel 28 is doing a documentary on me and we had cameras and sound men on the plane up and during the reading and on the plane back, so forth so forth. I felt like your Tom Jones although I didn't get anybody in the crapper.

actually, tho, ART is the matter, the crux, and with all the shit going on I keep this in my head, the real ACT, the form, the holiness. I love women but they are hardly the center of the universe.

I've suggested to Liza that she play it looser this time, keep some backups. She's going to the movies tonight with some guy. it's o.k. with me. I don't want to ever leave her totally ALONE again. they tell me she had a rough go when I was with Linda. also if I can get her to go out with men, then when I want to see somebody – say for a night or a couple of hours – I will be able to do so. say somebody like you.

Linda broke in while I was at Liza's last night and stole her sculpture of me back. That's all right, I trotted one of her paintings over and put it on her front porch. As long as I don't get murdered here, everything will be fine.

I read at Univ. of Ariz. on the 28th. Liza will prob. fly out with me. I don't know if the cameras will be along on this wing. It's a little different situation. U. of A. is rather uptight and I won't be able to drink very much. will prob. make a dull reading. I also have a tentative date at Cal State Long Beach Nov. 29, once at noon and again at night. If I'm still alive.

Yes, yes, I'm "hot to trot" to meet you. Your photo fine, fine! I might say I'm in love but how can you fall in love with a photo? and when I'm 52 and the photo's 27? You'll probably be disgusted when you meet me. I'm not a very good talker; in fact, a rather dull fellow.

Luck with your new love, but remember that few people hold up over the long run. Weaknesses begin to appear all over shit. It depends upon how much weakness you can love along with the good parts. It's good you keep shopping. The only way you can know what you have is by comparison.

Should we get together a bit it might be better if you come out here. (You almost found the way once.) We could go to a bar for a few, then maybe come to my place and have some drinks and talk. I live in a *very* beat-up front court. I am lazy and a shitty housekeeper. But there is great freedom here. The landlord and landlady are my friends and overlook a great many of my inconsistencies. Somehow your letters get me horny. Is it the pink paper? Not that we need make it. I don't want to do anything that you don't want to do.

You make my mailbox warm. Lemmee hear words from you . . .

[To Patricia Connell]
September 22, 1972

a short one until later – very hectic here – you won't believe it – I'm back with Linda. it's my last move. if I break with her it has to be somebody new. this going back and forth doesn't get it, it's cowardice. for a few days I was with one in the daytime, the other at night. now it's Linda. very stormy with Linda, but the love is high high high there, both physically and spiritually . . .

I haven't been doing my work, so must get into it. Univ. of Ariz. next week. not a drop off the typer.

Linda's very violent. She kicked down my door in S.F., clawed my face, bit a hole in my arm. But what love we make together! She's 32.

This is just to let you know that I am still together, it's hardly a letter; will write when I have more time.

Yes, you got left alone on your own doing . . . left with the tv tube, but I'm happy for you that you were able to have a few drinks and write to me, for you weren't entirely alone then, and you know me well enough to let loose a few things. I wonder which of our love-life's the most fucked-up? You with all your beauty and youth, you have troubles too. me, I'm extra emotional, my mind's half gone, I expect trouble, I may even create it. But with your equipment you should have things under control.

well, listen, my invisible love out there, I really have some WORK to do. keep touch. I'll write again if I'm alive.

[To Patricia Connell]
October 2, 1972

It rather cheered the old man up to talk to you today, all these low dark clouds, and somehow you got me to laughing. I guess that reading at the Univ. of Ariz. looped me down. such a staid gang . . . afterwards there was a reception . . . cookies and some kind of lemon punch . . . Christ, and me with my tongue hanging out . . . I mean for a *drink*, Connell, a drink . . .

yes, the sculpt. is a looker, a vamp, a tease . . . a bitch . . . a schitzy, and, at times, a wonderful woman. I don't suppose it will ever be smooth with us and I don't suppose I'll ever stop breaking up with her. but it does me good to break off from her because it gives me more area. but, I must admit, this last get-together, it was my idea, I did the work, I did the talking . . . but we're still always on explosive ends. the male-female relationship is almost impossible, yet one keeps looking, trying . . . so many things fuck it up, small things really, like not getting together on a Thursday night . . . some small offhand thing can crash it all down. nerves, maybe. or looking for an edge. it all seems to keep crashing. and it's not just me; I look around and everybody is in trouble. and now what am I doing writing a 27 years old woman? you're 25 years younger than I. I gotta be crazy. but I guess we ought to have a drink together sometime just so we can laugh each other off. you might think, why that ugly old dog, what'd he think he was gonna do? and I'd think, why, that stewardess, she ain't got no SOUL like me. you know. something.

Liza I did wrong to and there's no excuse, except I know that if somebody dumps me now I have no need to cry in my beer – I'll be getting just what I gave.

How are all your loves going? You may have too much going at once. It might make it lively but it might make it hard to level off so you can see where you are. It's almost impossible to have a steady relationship going with one man while carrying on side relationships with others. Me? I'm different. I'm the dirty old man. I can do what I want.

I got an offer for a reading in Canada. Do Eskimos really kiss with their noses? What else do they do?

ta ta, this is your invisible lover.

[To Carl Weissner]
October [?3], 1972

[* * *] Made the San Fran reading, 800 at 2$ a head, I got $400. I suppose there were various expenses. They put a refrig. full of beer on stage with me. After a while I mostly stopped reading and sat there drinking beer. Split with sculptress up there, went back to Liza. Then split with Liza, went back to sculptress. At moment am with sculptress. There's no rest, there's no victory, there's no meaning, and love comes in salt-grain size. Well, you know this.

There's this airline stewardess, 27, maybe she's the one. Maybe I can drag her ass down to the Bukowski depths. but the sculpt has quite a hold on me; maybe not as good a hold as she had 6 months ago, but it is some kind of hold.

Speaking of a "hold," there seems to be a hold on my writing now. Is this the end, old buddy? Has Bukowski coughed it up? I'd suppose not. I suppose it will be along. No telling, though. That's what makes the madness good.

[* * *] Maybe I'm just a drunk. You know, you get with the female, they get on you for the drinking. I suppose I do act the ass when I'm

drinking, but there's a necessary release there. I get out into this available space that is always there to float in. No, it doesn't make any sense to anybody but me. But it puts me somewhere, and when I get back down I walk to the typewriter and the keys work better. But drinking, to the female, really violates something in them. THEY HATE IT WORSE THAN ANOTHER WOMAN. It might kill you, they say, we love you. But they don't figure it might kill me a thousand other different ways to remain sober and drink tea. ah ah ah well.

[To John Martin]
October 8, 1972

Now that you're thinking of bringing out a collection of my columns — stories — you needn't feel like my energies are being taken by somebody else. I rather like to earn that hundred and a half if possible. How about the title? Can I cut loose on that too?

I still need to work with my old pal the poem, tho, and I enclose a few more. The novel? Well, I believe it will awaken soon . . . faith, faith. Everything must work by itself. I don't know why I tell you these things — you already know them. Hello to Barbara. yes, yes.

old 52, Henry Charles

p.s. — I'm on the comeback trail. Linda seems to inspire me *when* things are going well. B.

[To Gerard Malanga]
October 27, 1972

Man, you know, I am under it too, under all that any of us are. this doesn't mean I am too weak to respond, but basically I am fucked . . . I mean, fucked with what I am and how to work it and not work it.

Signs, counter-signs keep working, they keep working me, I don't know how to work them. there's neither humility or artistry here (in me), it's just a working of a process and it is more clever than I am.

I've gone through, I think, plenty, but there'll be plenty more.

I suppose this all sounds very holy. I am supposed to be the tough guy, the battered Bogart with a typewriter. that's their idea.

there's very little to subsist upon. all this grist we are supposed to create an art upon. sometimes I think that the greatest creators have been the greatest liars. well, inventiveness, that counts, doesn't it?

too precious, too precious, I know.

well, shit, hang in.

Copyright by Charles Bukowski.

[To Carl Weissner]
December 7, 1972

[* * *] I am still in this female battle, and I can't quite figure it, they are entirely too clever for me. it rips me up and makes me late answering to good people like you who are only trying to keep me together and you together while trying to make whipcream out of mudshit. (Life, ya know.) I never met a guy who fought harder for me while getting as little via $$$$ so I just know you've got to like what I am writing down in a line of words.

all right, I say let's get it all going. I wrote Ferling to accept all offers, but he is strange, he runs hot, he runs cold, yet I can't bitch he put out a fat book of my screams. whether he likes me personally is another matter, it doesn't matter because it's my work I'm selling not my drunken days and nights and fits and panics and dreamatics [sic], swans with knotted necks singing Elvis Presley . . . [* * *]

like I say, I'm sorry I'm so long on this answering but you know what a woman (women) can do to a man. at 52 I've taken some guts shots that my mind (and experience) should have warned me to ward off. not that I'm crying: maybe that piece of my soul that was blown off needed to be. but it all weakens energy and is a pissing upon my barricades. so much for excuses . . . I don't know if I've said anything relevant here, but the two bottles of beer were good, and I still remember the unexpected birthday gift, the cigars and the bottle. I've kept the box. I'm soft on that kind of shit. and feel justified being that way. I hope your life isn't going too bad. Tell Andernach I said hello.

Martin had been urging Bukowski to write an autobiographical novel based on his childhood but Bukowski found the memories too painful. Several short stories based on this material had been published in Confessions of a Man Insane Enough to Live With Beasts *and some more would follow in his book of short stories* South of No North.

[To John Martin]
December 16, 1972

on the novel, you know, shit, we stumble. I've decided that I must enclose parts that were printed in earlier mimeo editions to fill out parts. otherwise, it can't be done properly. yet the writing will be different, better. I do believe I am writing better than ever. how long this will hold has much to do with the gods and luck and the way I walk down the street. o.k. so I'll start the novel up again. I've hardly felt like writing the immortal novel, maybe I never will. if I do I'll probably be 65 or 70 or 80. I think of some of Hamsun's tomes. he did some living. that has to be there first. I suppose that's the trouble with professional writers — they become so professional they stop living. well, I mean they live as writers, consciously live that way, they stop living haphazardly as humans. well, I don't like humans or writers but I think I'm still loose, I'm not a professional writer and if I ever become one I promise you first boot at my ass, hemorrhoids and all. yeh, they're back. o, yes. poems enclosed.

p.s. — I get good rays off your Robert Kelly, he is basically a good sort although he has maneuvered himself into a strange area where it becomes more button than bone. he reminds me of a big dog heavy with water that he wants to shake off. but he's kind, that counts. I think he wants to sing on and on, throw words like pebbles. that's all right, you know. he's a little too holy but most of us are . . .

[To John Martin]
December 29, 1972

[* * *] got your good check today. It's a lifeblood thing and always appreciated. I suppose I'm into you for a bit now but maybe it will work your way, finally. I think the writing has gotten better since I got out of the post office — except for the first frantic months . . .

Creeley's all right. He's been sniped at too long. We've got to allow him an occasional tantrum or bitterness. the rancor that's out there is unbelievable. I rather enjoy their knocks but that's because I'm a little punchy. That is, I don't mind their knocks when they are published in magazines or newspapers, so forth for everybody to see. what I object to is little hate letters, little jealousy letters to Linda about me from various mimeo editors and poets (?) . . . meanwhile, look at their poems, and who are they trying to write like? ta, ta.

[★ ★ ★] you tell Barbara that I'm still punching this machine. Harry Truman's gone, Ezra's gone, but I'm still here. laying down the line.

• 1973 •

[To A. D. Winans]
January 18, 1973

Excuse the delay but I've come off a 4 day drunk that damn near did it all the way . . . still shaky . . . but alive. I'll get some work to you soon for your project. I've changed my mind on answering my critics. I did that in the last *Holy Doors* bit and I think one can only go so far in answering that way . . . it gets you down there wallowing in all that shit: kind of like a COSMEP conference. I'll just let them have their say, all right? by the way, I'm *honored*, if I didn't say so before, to have a special issue [of *Second Coming*] on this Charles Bukowski guy. [* * *]

[To Joanna Bull]
January 19, 1973

It's bad to be down but we all get down, I get down all the time. Break-ups are bad because 2 people just don't realize how much they fill in for each other until the bust-up, then you feel it all. There's no advice I can give or no wisdom. I drink when I'm down but it only makes it worse. I suppose you'll make it through – women are tougher than men.

I could come by to see you some night. Wednesday night is a good time. But it would just be talk. I'm 52 anyhow, and been going with a 32 year old sculptress-writer. We have some hard times but basically I feel like playing her fair. Not that I mean we'd fuck or such anyhow. just to mention, I could drop by . . . where the hell's Ocean Front Walk?

Thanks the poem . . . You speak of reading a book. one of mine. which one?

I've been in a writing slump of late. I mean I haven't written for a week. no, I wrote a column last night. I forgot. I had a fight with Linda. Confusing.

I don't know. the human being is really durable. I've actually felt pain crawling all over me like a dark skin, meanwhile the same motherfucking shimmering knife in the gut in the gut in the gut in the gut . . . again and again. but sometimes durability ends. I tried one suicide and failed. gas.

and a new involvement hardly ever solves an old involvement. there's no escape, and damned little hope. but we have to laugh. jesus we have to laugh.

as far as writing goes, other writers, they don't come through much to me. it may be ego. I've got tons of ego and tons of self-doubt. I'm in good shape.

you hang in,
Buk

[To John Martin]
January 23, 1973

Iz u still alive? don't worry about the novel, the novel is taking another breather. the fat must stoke up and then I will skim it off. you understand: everything at its proper time. meanwhile, some more poems. I hope you and Creeley have patched up your broken knitting.

everybody's dying – Truman, Johnson, some old jazz great today at 87 . . . name slides past . . . we are still working the keys. My master plan is to live to be 80 but that last drunk damn near did me in. I can handle a one night drunk but if I hang 2 or 3 of them together my system just can't take it. I'm 52. that doesn't mean I have to stop living but it does mean that some of the living must be channeled away from the old bottle. I think too many writers have let it eat them up, kill them. if I can hang in 28 more years of fair writing, I'll be satisfied. don't forget, I rather more or less began at 35 so they owe it to me on this end. o.k. let's see what happens.

[To John Martin]
March 8, 1973

[* * *] listen, I have the most expensive dentist in town. I don't know where I found him. he has these nurses that crawl all over you (me), rub up against one (me) with tit and flank, stare deeply (platitude) into eye (mine). this costs (me). in the old days they called them dentists, you walked in, opened your mouth, stuck your finger in there, said "get that one." you sat down and he yanked it out. now they're called dental surgeons, have these prostitutes around, you just get hard-ons — no teeth pulled. consultations, x-rays, clever jokes. an appointment once a month. meanwhile you're charged and nothing done. also I lost at the track the other day. [* * *]

I checked out Eshleman's poem on the spider. do you realize that he is invading my sacred and private grounds? my poems are full of spiders. spiders, horses, beer and gentle and innocent lament.

[To Carl Weissner]
March 23, 1973

Well, it's all not so bad here, I'm drinking a bottle of calif. rhine wine — cheap shit, granted, but not too cheap — smoking a rolled Prince Albert (and I still can't type) . . . we waste some time playing the horses but not too much money . . . I'm waiting for the Muse to grow giant-size. . . . Linda wrote a one-act play, pretty good too, it'll be on the boards in May, I think. no cash but a start. I've gotten some $$$$ offers to do a play but maybe I can't do a play and I just don't want to limp in with some lines . . . the force and the mood just gotta precede me. there are some wars here with the lady but then I'm a little crazy in my thinking, or maybe I'm not crazy in my thinking. anyhow, I'm still here, it's a good change, and I'm not going to say LOVE too heavy because that might jinx it. [* * *]

as I write this Linda stands by the typewriter reading over my shoulder and scratching her beautiful ass. now she laughs. now she rattles papers. now she rattles papers and laughs.

now she says Bukowski will you please shut up about me? she's such a modest kid.

o.k. she says the book of the year is hers not mine, and it's called *Sweet and Dirty*. and it is. maybe I can get her to send you a free autographed copy. o.k.?

where was I?

all right, I've got to get into some work, work, work, but I hardly think of it as work especially after a long layoff (6 or 7 days) the words build and the ideas climb like hornets about the walls, ah. the divinity of our lives is majorly amazing . . .

I must roll another cigarette and watch the blue smoke curl and curl and curl and let myself feel good for a few moments. I never used to let myself feel too good. now, for some reason, I feel like I deserve to feel good. I've paid the baker, the druggist, the gods, the cops, the pimps and the whores . . . now, look – see how it works? Linda just came over and got some of my wine. a little shot, she says. little? there went half a bottle . . .

Love Story. yes, I saw it on tv. I never laughed so much in my life. what a ridiculous hunk of pretentious phoney shit but looking at it as pure comedy it was magnificent, if you know what I mean. I guessed each scene before it arrived. you know, the world is really a long long way from solving ANYTHING when they gulp in this kind of tripe and admire it. no chance, friend. we might as well give up. just saw off a corner of the action, a very tiny corner and sit there and wait for them to come and get us. [★ ★ ★]

[To A. D. Winans]
March 23, 1973

Listen, here is a photo of me. Didn't you want a photo of me? o.k., here's one. is the Bukowski issue still on? I want to get famous.

When do you want me to start working on a cover idea? How much porno can you handle? when in the hell are you coming out with this issue? summer? will I live until summer? I think I'll get a statement of sorts to you. I think maybe a longer statement, bio and rambling, will be better than a short story. I'll get a couple of bottles of wine and sit down one night to the typer. we'll get many imperfections that way but I'm not against imperfections. I think that the literary people are too smooth too careful, cover mistakes. we'll piss on that. all right? after all, it's *my* old ass that is going to be exposed. . . . [★ ★ ★]

[To A. D. Winans]
April 2, 1973

sounds like you did it up but there you go, it's the price and pain of drinking and it's like the price and pain of women — you've got to pay hard sometimes when you least expect it. I've been in so much trouble, jail jail jail jail jail jail jail jail jail jail and fine, fine and jail, drunk driving, getting beat up while drunk, all that, well, it's the same for most of us but one of the best things I learned *was to stay out of the bars* and also to try to stay off the street. I fail sometimes to stay off the streets but not too often. the finest place on earth to drink is in your own place and *alone*. you probably know all this. all right. [* * *]

so now look I've got to scrape myself together and work the typewriter ribbon a bit. some real dead creeps over last night, brought no energy, and I had to split with the beer though there were 4 of them. taken again. they ate my time. nothing to do, they had nothing to do, and there are billions like them.

[To John Martin]
April [?25], 1973

[* * *] they're rough on the P's lately. Picasso gone, Pound gone, it's hardly false humility when I say I'm not in their class, but it's still good going on a while, working with the word and the way. there's no other life and when I realize and look back on all those years working for other men for their way and their profit and their glowing beings, I realize that this is a very magic and lucky time, indeed indeed indeed, and you had very much to do with making it so. sometimes I awaken at night and think, my wrists are here, I'm here, my toes, my body, there's the walls and there are the streets outside, dark hard blood-tasting streets, I know them. And I think, just a few years more like this and I'll be paid back for all of it. well, now we have been very somber and serious. let's let up. you balding red-haired devil, don't get run over in the streets, I won't know which way to look.

[To Joanna Bull]

May 1, 1973

I'm still living with Linda. Some rough battles. I don't know if we're going to make it. I don't know whose fault it is. Some of it might be mine, but not entirely.

Anyhow, Linda makes her annual trek to Utah around mid-June, stays about 3 weeks, and I'd like to see you a few times then. I have good memories of you – so far. So, around mid-June, if you're still there I'll try to contact you. I hope you're still there. We needn't push too hard at each other. I have nothing to prove. It's just that I feel that the Linda situation won't hold up, and it would be good to know somebody. I have male friends but it's hardly the same thing. You be happy if possible.

"SPR" is the Small Press Review *published quarterly by Dustbooks from Paradise, California, from 1967 to 1974, and later as a monthly. Nikos Stangos was the editor of the Penguin Contemporary Poets series, in which Bukowski shared a volume with Harold Norse and Philip Lamantia.*

[To A. D. Winans]

May 16, 1973

I think the SPR was a hatchet job to begin with, Fulton leading the tribe. I don't mind Norse; I think he's truly mixed-up on what has occurred, he's basically honest and stung, it's just that the eyes that see out of him or whatever sees out has it wrong. It's like Martin said when he read Norse, "But, Jesus, you *told* me to print him!" Al, things happen to us all and when things don't work we tend to point to others. I've been in the same room with Norse when he has made his accusations to me and they were so out of the way and ridiculous that I didn't respond except to take another drink. I still think Norse is a fine poet but he has become a great big grandma weeping into the towel. I don't know what to do with him. I suppose the best thing to do with him is just to let him go on writing his poems while I write mine. His claim that he got me into Penguin 13 might have some truth. He was a friend of Stangos, one of the editors. If I wanted to be a bitch I might suggest that Norse got in the same way. But I'm sure that Stangos and Penguin and Norse himself wouldn't have wanted me if I hadn't shown them a good spitter, a good slider and a fair fast ball.

I thought Packard did a good professional job, and Linda King's was amusing and Quag's was drab o.k. but most of the others were in with some kind of buildup or bitch or grind, trying to make a climb upon the Buk myth or mystique or Buk bullshit or whatever. It was an attempt at a personal advancement of sorts – saying: if he's no good and I know he's no good, I *must* be good, even great. It's all right. Watergate poetry. These tiny shit climbers bug me, hahaha. Winans, too much time used upon talking about them gives them what they need. I don't want to go into them or out of them anymore. Except to say, that frankly, it's not bad being attacked, it was expected. long ago, when I first started writing poems at age 35 to Jon Webb: "I know when I get them angry that I am getting there." These aren't the exact words. I just went over to the bookcase to find them but didn't want to bother. Tra la la.

[* * *] listen, criticism is all right – if they can break it down and say it's wrong and why – I think I did that with my review of Hemingway's last book *Islands in the Stream* for *TV and Fine Arts Guide*. There is a way of doing things, but the cheap shots never pay off. I have given a few low shots – for sake of caricature – but not too many cheap ones have I dealt. I don't run cheap; I keep it strong and clipped and even, and that's what pisses them.

I am glad that there are *some* littles that play something besides the lonely heart and diminutive talent game. these few show that there's a chance somewhere in all of us, a human easy decent chance. that's plenty, that little chance. the whole god damned nation of the United States of America is now wobbling. failing, failing, with all that power. think of how some 19 year old kid in his mother's bedroom, just getting over acne and going to college and having his 25 buck Sears Roebuck mimeo machine sitting there must feel? he can reject Ginsberg if he wants to because Ginsberg likes to send to such shit rags. 25 dollars doesn't make an editor, though it can. there are just too many non-things playing as things. I do suppose it's the age of superfluousness. everybody is something, or thinks they are. what a vast can of *shit*. how are we ever going to get out of it? – meanwhile, while I write this I'm not writing something else. [* * *]

[To Joanna Bull]
July 1, 1973

All right, after the first week in July I'll phone and see if I might come by with my tiny bottle of beer.

Things very tenuous here. I once loved Linda very much and I believe she still loves me (love is an easy word to use here for lack of something else) but it is slowly breaking off, it has to be final, eventually. I don't want to break your back with my side of the story. Perhaps, someday, I can write it down – novel form. Somerset Maugham wrote something near to it, but hardly near enough and he seemed to lean towards homosexual proclivities and I think it takes a man to write about a woman. A woman can't do it either, and maybe not me. It's so difficult to tread center in the female-male Emote. But I am obsessed with the Art-form, it's the only religion, the only beastly breath of air left. It purifies shit, it explains it; it lets you sleep at night, finally. I'm not a moralist and I don't believe in conscience but in matters of feeling one should be careful. I am careful because feelings are holy and humorous and three-quarters of the sun. I don't trust the mind unless it's run by the bellybutton . . . god, how I go on! what am I saying? I said that I wouldn't break your back.

I suppose with Linda I filled the father-fixation process or whatever the fuck you call it? Ask the Calif. School of Psychology. Are you ready for a father-fixation process? My darling beautiful Linda goes into all manners of fits and fandangos when I reject her final innards and make moves to leave – mostly violent, very, physical attacks which I handle as best I may. Which means getting her under control with as little injury to her as possible. I am what you call a very cool cat under fire. Some other men would have killed her long ago; I am looking for material for a novel, and I once did love her; besides she came out of a madhouse and they haven't put me into one, yet. That makes me master, doesn't it?

Look, you say obsessions die hard with you? Is that what men are? Obsessions? Don't you ever want to give up the game of hurt and hunt and chess and cheat? Can't you make a value judgment? Can't you choose anybody? To lay down with and look at the ceiling with and listen to music and smoke cigarettes and talk and laugh and flow? Wouldn't it feel good to you to become something? Shit, I'm not saying it's me. I'm your father. But it should be somebody. Somebody for somebody, even if it's only yourself. That's what I'm working on: me for me, easy at first, and then maybe I can open a door for somebody else.

[To John Martin]
July 4, 1973

Well, shit, I don't know, I'm heading for some foolish Utah mountain, I might be gone from two to four weeks and I suppose there might not be much work done. Linda wins again. But don't worry. I'm making a study on her. If I ever get it down right some day you'll see the female exposed as she has never been exposed. Very difficult to do, though; the tone of the writing must be impartial, exact. The more it's that way the better it will be. meanwhile, haha, there's still *Factotum*, isn't there? [★ ★ ★]

[To A. D. Winans]
July 16, 1973

been on a week's beerdrunk, back from Utah, Linda and I have split, I have to be out of here by the 29th. I've got a little book with 3 or 4 numbers but I'll be damned if I quite want to get involved again, maybe never again, kid, I'll be 53 in August, and this battling with and living with the female has kept me trim in a fashion, but so much of the game is run on trickery, chess moves, false moves, ticklers, blasters, farts and one-tenth feelings . . . Ugh, I'm too simple to comprehend, understand . . . I think most of our women have been raised too much upon movie magazines and the screen. They've learned game-playing and dramatics but my head just wants to go where it is.

yes, run the Norse, I haven't had a good belly-tickler in some months. I think that what has happened with Hal is that he has put total importance upon *poetics* and what a poet is supposed to be. a good poet never knows what he is, he's a dime from the edge, but there's nothing holy about it. it's a job. like mopping a bar floor. I can't rail too much against him; I suppose that the things he has imagined in his mind seem very true to him. who is the judge? I rattled around his place in Venice a couple of nights drunk but it was much more in energy and clowning than malice or a wish to destroy. I'm an asshole in many ways, I even enjoy my assholeness. I can tear a man in half in a short story; I can also tear myself in half, but I'm no knifer, I don't whisper things into editors' ears. I'm no destroyer. Nothing can be destroyed that has the power to move forward into its own thing. fame or acceptance or politics or power has nothing to do with it. nothing is needed but self going-on as self must. one only need realize this small realization. [* * *]

Mich[eline] is all right – he's one third bullshit but he's got a special divinity and a special strength. [* * *] I can't think of another poet who has more and who has been neglected more. Jack is the last of the holy preachers sailing down Broadway singing the song. He's right: they'll find him after he's dead. [* * *] Jack has it; through all the bullshit and con and hollering, Jack has it. may the gods give him a good woman who understands him, and a better Age to live in than this castrated, de-emphasized, titless, toothless, anti-human, anti-word, anti-feeling 20th century, amen.

the split with Linda isn't easy. I never go into things with just a toenail. but we can't fall down on the rug and die. we came up too hard and too slow. we are dumb but not quite damned. and most of the things that happen to each of us happen to everybody. not that it lessens the feelings but we have to keep remembering that we aren't especially singular or especially precious. [* * *]

think how low we'd feel without even the word to bounce around? well, there's beer and a rolled cigarette and my radio plays a touch of Brahms. I haven't grown much. I don't know how.

[To Carl Weissner]
August 11, 1973

sorry the silence but as you can see I'm at a new address, Linda and I have split and I am a little bit out of my brain, guts dangling . . . [* * *]

I am really down low. can't even get the word down. forgive.

[To Carl Weissner]
September 10, 1973

sorry I dripped the blues on you last letter, I've got the pieces put together better now, still trouble, trouble with women and trouble inside of my head, but I guess that all the rumbling and shit and insanity counts, let's hope so. if I ever get stable I might as well sell my ass to the peacocks. [* * *]

actually, though, I do have my UPS. I sometimes sit around thinking, god, some people think that I am a writer. How did I ever fool them? I can't write a cat's turd. I am still alive. I can lay in this bed for 4 days and nobody will bother me. That's fine. I can masturbate, I can kill myself. dear god, I have all kinds of freedoms. I can even read *The Rebel* by Camus, that book I bought the other day at Martindales except I lost my glasses the last time I was drunk and I can't read the print. I verily can even open a can or bottle of beer.

all right, baby, the hard rain falls for all of us sometime. take Job. take him a long ways away. I am tired of his wails. take me a long way away.

you hold too. all this lightning, she gotta stop.

[To A. D. Winans]
October 7, 1973

listen, Micheline did get me at a bad time. Some of the stories were all right but he does get too much into this MOON — GLORY — I AM A POET trip and it tends to sink the whole thing. like, poor bastard, he's a poet. well, there are a lot of poor bastards — interns in hospitals, garbage collectors, dishwashers, factory workers, farm hands . . . if anybody has divine rights they probably have them too.

[To A. D. Winans]
October 24, 1973

you write a letter like a man who knows where it's at.

yeh, we all come out of areas. Lefty O'Doul. boy, what a hitter. he was an old man when he was managing the Seals but he still pinch hits against the Angels down here, and damn, every time I saw him it seemed he got his hit . . . but, like you, all that has drained for me. you keep seeing them coming and going and there are all the screams and then it vanishes. I think Ezra played a better game even though he denied it at the end. I think he realized he played it a little too fancy and too heavy but he had guts enough to admit it and realize it.

getting over the documentary BUKOWSKI and making love to the ribbon again. I, shit yes, look forward to your special Buk edition, and with that maybe I can get back to the holy grind (poetry). ah.

you appear on the right road in. beware the blood-suckers. beware the friends. beware, especially, the poets. even me.

[To Gerald Locklin]
December 5, 1973

Well, readings are like women, they're good and they're bad, and you go on to the next one or you give them up altogether. But readings are only an aid to survival and I can't in anyway judge them as a creative act. It's closer to carnival and you need some luck and a few drinks to come out close to even. I think even guys like J. Dickey know this; he charges two grand, reads once or twice and goes out and shoots something with a bow and arrow. A man needs his basic strength in order to move that typewriter ribbon into good action. The idea of the game must never be forgotten: the laying down of the line.

The '49-er bar is as close to literary bar as anything I have seen; but, luckily, it ain't snob, the rays are good and easy. Now I gotta fly up to S.F. and do my little act. I pretty much feel like a whore selling quicky snatch up an alley. Well, it beats being middle linebacker for the The Dallas Cowboys. [★ ★ ★]

• 1974 •

These two young writers had founded a magazine entitled Aunt Harriet's Flair for writing Review, *only one issue of which appeared, November 1974.*

[To James Whitaker and Ebenezer Juarez]
January 3, 1974

got your ten. hot cha. you've got an immortal title to your mag. the problem is in setting the pages on fire. I know. I edited a mag once. 3 issues. I dwarfed out. just not enough around. o.k. I wrote these poems yesterday. look them over. let me know, plus or minus. I still got your motherhumpin' ten. you seem to show style. do send me your first issue whether I'm in it or not.

p.s. – you needn't drop a check on him because unlike me he's got money and *plenty*, but it hasn't seemed to diminish his humanism (whatever that is) or his artistry (whatever that is) but I'd suggest you write him for some poems . . . he can lay the line down: Steve Richmond [*address follows*].

[To James Whitaker]
January 14, 1974

help, help, help, help, help, now LISTEN: tear up poem "sitting around listening to Bach"!!! wrote this on split with my woman, was bitter and vindictive; may be good writing in there but it definitely is from the wrong source, especially now . . . wouldn't want woman I'm back with to *read* that poem . . . DESTROY. I've destroyed my copy . . . stamped enclosed envelope to let me hear from you that you've done likewise, AND, I want to THANK YOU, MIGHTILY. o.k.?

no, haven't read anything by Jim Harrison; that isn't saying that he couldn't quite well have it, though.

the millionaire's daughter and I lived (for a while) in Wheeler, Texas ... the place with 7 lakes and wild turkey and *green woods* ... Frye Interceptor, World War II plane, planned and put together by her father. Gramps owned the land and the farmers did the work for ½ the profit while the son's planes sprayed the crops and were paid for it. on and on. like you know, we didn't make it. if I remember, Wheeler very near to Oklahoma border and voted by a panel of experts as the last place in U.S. anybody would care to lay an atomic bomb upon.pop. then about 2,000. [★ ★ ★]

[To A. D. Winans]
January 21, 1974

Went to the p.o box today and there it was – Vol. 11, no. 3. I don't go to the box often, don't know how long it has been laying there, but to let you know – much more solid than *The Small Press Review.* better writers writing. I guess it *was* needed to get some of the grit out. I think the best part was that most saw me for what I was – fucked-up, battered, battering, punchy but durable, trying to get out, trying to get it on down. Literature has always had this sheen of dignity, it's disgusting. I'm glad if we put some dirt and blood on the carpet. even those who were always crying for a changed literature, a better literature, a more *real* thing, guys like Pound and W. C. Williams, they *still* worked out of the formal, stilted cage. I hope we've now gotten some freedom for those who follow. Maybe I carry it too far. for instance, I've always advocated that they serve beer, play music, maybe have strippers at our museums. think of how much better *and* more real the sabre tooth tiger would look? o.k., you know what I mean.

I liked the Richmond. He knows how to give due to the object without destroying the object involved. this is no easy thing. Steve also knows how to write a *sentence*. Most can't. [★ ★ ★] I have said for years that Steve Richmond is the most underrated human and writer and painter that I know. perhaps it's best that way. he's protected. he may be lucky too if they leave him alone. a man must have time to build certain walls so if they finally come with their pompoms he can take that, and still go on.

Micheline was fine, god damn romantic hustler, he turned on high, he sings those lines, he's in rhythm and breaking through. [★ ★ ★] when Jack is turned on high he is capable of writing a better poem than I could ever write. I write more good poems over the long haul but when he is totally high and singing I can't touch him. if he stays at it and stops hounding the publishers and just does his work he will be found again long before he is dead. [★ ★ ★]

Norse? I understand his viewpoint. we simply come out of different poetic backgrounds. [★ ★ ★] And when I'm drunk I am generally rude and boorish and stupid to everybody alike. I just don't select Hal. If he could understand this he might feel better. before a man can ever meet the gods he must learn to forgive the drunks. [★ ★ ★]

Alta. I understand her viewpoint and it certainly must seem plausible and right to her, but creation, art, is the breakthrough. we hardly do what is proper or kind, though often, in life, we are kinder than most, much more. without flying flags about it. Alta does not know how to write a sentence down. it hurts her pitch. I don't want to rape Alta. I don't want to rape anybody. I never have. But if an artist wants to go into the mind of a rapist or a murderer and look out of that mind and write down that mind, I don't think that is criminal. furthermore, I didn't say my stories in *NOLA* were "sarcastic." I don't apologize for my work. If I write a story about a shitty woman then that shitty woman did exist. one form or another. blacks can also be shitty as can whites. I refuse to be restricted in the materials I can paint with. it's really all so ridiculous to defend anything as *just* that thing, can't they even understand that? Oh, Alta, I *have* love . . . that's why I can write of other things. [★ ★ ★]

Hugh Fox, as usual, uses the opportunity to advertise himself. that's all right. if you got the talent to back up your breakthrough. see: Hemingway–Fitzgerald. When Fox claimed he had been beat about more physically than I had, that's untrue. [★ ★ ★] no man knows what a physical beating is until he gets one. getting off your knees in a dark alley with 14 drunks watching and before you can get your hands up to your knees he lands again and gives you a knee in the nuts as you go down. Nothing to do but get up. finally it becomes a matter of breathing. you can hardly breathe. and neither can the man who is murdering you. and finally, as you start to come back on him, they stop the fight. you get in 7 or 9 of these, you know what a physical beating is. and the factories and the farm labor market. Fox is a dreamer. he's never had a physical beating. I looked at his face. he still hasn't had one. I can tell by the way he writes.

All in all, Al, it was a very good issue, and the stuff I wrote and the way I lived was mostly for me, but I see that if some have picked up a certain style and meaning in it, good. But I never mean my way to be their way. they can have theirs and I don't think they'd fit in mine. that's fair. I do much of my stuff out of tune, out of one ear. we don't want a mythology or a hero. it was just a way to go. and there's still tomorrow. Shakey's tomorrow &&&&&&. then Dashiel H's, or was it somebody else's Big Sleep. ah, hahaha. after I'm dead Hal Norse will be able to eat his softboiled eggs and his Egyptian parsley in peace.

[To Carl Weissner]
May 17, 1974

I got the *Gedichte die einer schrieb* . . . your signed copy, plus 5 others from the publisher. You put it together so well, babe, you make me feel like Bogart Bukowski Bukowski Bukowski. I like it. I like to like things sometimes. You know I've gone a hard route and have put down some words and you don't mind admitting it. all right, it has been a good circus, and I'm lucky to have you over there to transmute me. ah. the book has the warm feel of burning and there. you've done it. You know you have. I won't brag anymore on the book – except to say the good things you've done for me usually arrive at times when I need them most. Like you know, hahaha, I am rifting with my woman again; it is such a slow process, these many breakups, but it's necessary to finalize it finally. the woman's thoughts and feelings are continually against mine and the other way around. she seems to understand my enemy more than she does me, so there's only one thing left to do – let her go to the enemy. it's not easy, but she belongs with them; I've only borrowed something from them. tra, la. tra, la.

Big shoot-out tonight. I guess it happened just as I left the racetrack, a loser, after the 9th race. I passed very close. The SLA[1] Army, it seems. Trying to look for some symphony music on the radio I passed upon the news. Nothing finalized at this moment. But much fire-power. Where they were holed-up caught on fire. There are so many angles to this thing.

---

1. The "Symbionese Liberation Army," a terrorist group best remembered for kidnapping Patty Hearst and converting her to their cause.

One is that DeFreeze was allowed to escape from a minimum security area when he was in jail. whoever knows that and what the truth is? who knows who squealed? Who knows who is who? Who knows what it finally really means? Maybe just the tv screen brought into the streets? maybe an overdose of Marx? Christ knows I am one of the last who knows what's going on around here, and I hardly adore it. But I don't know if I love the SLA anymore than I do the USA. It's all a manner of hard hunger and wanting control. Each side pushes so hard that they become dehumanized. religion and the popular vote, of course, are the softeners. but, babe, I've got to believe that *we* are in the right slot — creation is the greatest and purest revolution of them all, and it finally causes everything else to move behind it. Maybe too far behind it. But we are the prow. we know the death and the waste and the glory, and some of the way, and we have Eye enough to see the Revolutionary, the Capitalist, the Fascist and the cabbage. We have trouble with women, but give us a new typewriter ribbon and some of the rent paid, we get the courage up, and getting the courage up and moving toward the sun, that's fair enough in this time of bending funnels.

since I got kicked out of the lady's house for not caring for her parties and my friends (she *likes* my friends), I came on over here, and there has been much trouble here, I inhale and they phone the police, I scratch myself and they beat on my floor (I'm up on the 2nd) and the little man came around and said, Inflation, gave me a notice of a rent boost and also my friends below and all those about this frog-in-the-garden-pond-vine-death-cement endurance of quiet posing and pissing and murders; how they HATE the sound of my typewriter . . . [★ ★ ★]

so the town is half burning down again over here. and I'm *still* on my second novel . . . Let's hope that the German female and the German life is fairly good to you over there. if I ever get enough money, which I won't, I want to come over and see you, have you lead me down the streets of Andernach, I will weep and we will drink beer somewhere and my mouth will form into a round toothless and insensible hole, and you'll think, great god, what've I got on myself here? Bogart turned to mulch and butter. I shoulda translated Douglas Blazek.

Winans published Wantling's 7 on Style *in 1975. Bukowski's foreword was not included (see letters of July 25 to Weissner and November [?] to Winans, below).*

[To A. D. Winans]
May 21, 1974

Have been in bad mental state so have not responded to yours . . . sobered up now and on better spiritual grounds.

Yes, I know about Wantling, Ruthie phoned me about it some time back. Like, we're always ready for the death thing yet when it happens we're still not ready. I picked up on Bill, all the way. So, sure I'd like to do the foreword to *Style*. Wantling had been sending me some of the poems but I can't seem to locate them. If I do a foreword, of course, I'd like to see the poems. Can you manage to send me xerox copies? [★ ★ ★]

On Bergé, she's down on me. We had a bit of a haggle when I was editing *Laugh Literary*. Nothing much. She wrote what I thought to be a letter that was a bit precious when I rejected her poems. I mailed the letter back but she returned it. I had no recourse but to publish the letter. I guess she hasn't forgotten. She's never met me personally so her knowledge of me is through my writing. Enough. [★ ★ ★]

Bukowski is here reacting to an advance copy of Burning in Water, Drowning in Flame, *officially published June 21, 1974.*

[To John Martin]
June 17, 1974

I react slowly . . . it's my nature . . . but your (and Barbara's) (and my) Selected Poems book is a marvelous creature. I have not lost my wonderment toward very good things. Grace and luck to all of us. New poems enclosed.

[To A. D. Winans]
June 24, 1974

Well, here's the shot at it. I had to wait for it to pull together. If it doesn't work for you, send it back. See enclosed s.a.e.

I'm single again, trying different women. They're all pretty good if they don't stay over two days. [* * *]

Kitty Foyle *(1939) was a novel by Christopher Morley.*

[To John Martin]
July 16, 1974

on the Linda split – she could become the 3rd novel if I ever finish the 2nd. I don't know if I'm man enough to write it straight. S. Maugham did something similar – what was it? Kitty Foyle? No, something else, I believe. o.k. [* * *]

[To Carl Weissner]
July 25, 1974

[* * *] no, Prince, I don't take the ups and downs of women very good; I am a *very* emotional fellow, I get to like almost everything – even mosquitoes. one thing, though, I've never gotten much of an affinity of attachment for is the roach. only Kafka's marvelous roach, poor fellow. but I *do* take it hard because when I go, I throw away the oars. I know, I ought to know. hahaha. the female is generally *very* good to me. I haven't known a great many but most have been long runs. I'm not a chaser or a hunter. If one doesn't arrive, I don't search. But upon arrival, my guts generally go right down the mother drain, they're spilled in there, helplessly. I am tuned-up to this inside roar and when this inside roar touches upon something – it flicks off in a rather helpless state. it feels very good but the headlights are sometimes dim. what happened this last time is that I kept compromising in order to hold. she began to drift, at first, spiritually elsewhere because she thought she was beautiful and maybe she was,

but this type of woman needs constant outward attention from many outward sources. she needs feeding from many. I might need feeding from one, and when the chips are really down that one might only be me.

so there you had it. a Loner in bed next to one who needed the constant adulation of the Crowd. no way, Prince. the crowd drained me; it bucked her up like puffed wheat rice cereal dropped into milk. she found all manners of fascinating aspects about the crowd that to me only seemed pig-farts and creeping lies and game-playing and obviousness. she wanted parties, she wanted to dance and chat and giggle. she was Marilyn Monroe the sex pet, she modeled herself after her. she drove and whirled and gambled, wiggled her tits and ass, drove the men crazy. and I thought, christ, how did I ever get into this? it was simple: she had sought me out and I had sucked in. now she wanted me as the strong man springboard that she could leap off of and return to. she had her parties, she had her way. I held my ground, cooled it, looked the other way. she moved again. she started fucking guys, two in a week, followed quickly by another. same old shit – claiming she had only done it in reaction to me – the time she had caught my car outside Stella's house, the time I had gone with Liza Williams to Del Mar and slept along the shore with the waves breaking under us.

Prince, I found that she was too swift for me. She looked better than I did – to most people. She could get fucked more often and more continually. Does this sound like a bitch? She was. So she took off for Utah for 3 months and left me her television set. She told me that she would accept a Summer man but that I would be her Winter man and that it was only fair of her to tell her Summer man that.

How much shit can an old dog swallow? I wrote back and told her in three sentences that it was over. What the 3 sentences were don't matter here. but I cut the knot, Gordian or otherwise. it's finis. her tv is in her closet, the key is on the mantle and the birds piss into the wind, aloha. [★ ★ ★]

supposed to write foreword to one of Wantling's last books, *Style*. I did but his old lady came out here and we didn't make it at all – total opposites. It wasn't because I didn't fuck her, that wouldn't have been nec. It's only that all our ideas were reversed. I met and knew Wantling – we were on similar waves of a sort. Down in a motel in Laguna one night I snarled at his x-wife (death is divorce, isn't it?), "No wonder the son of a bitch had to take the needle for 9 years. He was living with you." Then I walked out drunk in my shorts and jumped to the bottom of the pool. came up. as you guessed. but at 54 I ought to wear water wings to pull shit like that. anyhow, she'll prob. nix the foreword, which is all right. I was only talking about *Style*. [★ ★ ★]

No, nobody has my tape. *Terror Street*. it has vanished into the languishing cunts that once spoke love. and there are a few new women about. I've fucked a few but the one I cared for I was afraid to fuck. I didn't want to make any mistakes. She had these rays shooting out about 30 feet from her body – I can't explain it, very difficult, she looked good but without push. everything I said she understood and I tried some wild areas. she got it, I could tell by her counter-answers. I left her alone. I let her sleep on my couch; I slept in my bed. neither of us slept all night. wide-awake. it was very funny. when I took her to the airport, everything was a generous high . . . no cancer. I'm going up to see her in August. I know that things are seldom as they seem, but I must find out . . . *again*. we're suckers to the last, Carl, cunt-suckers, soul-suckers. [* * *]

Carl, there has been a great emotional and spiritual spring-back since I cut myself loose from that Marilyn Monroe so-called good luck thing. she claimed that I restricted her artistic complexities. let her do well. you don't know how many of her poems I worked over to make them o.k. She'd read them to me. I'd say, "Now, look, don't you think you'd better just *drop* the 3rd line down? And the ending – what do you mean by that? It's useful to you but insensible to anybody else. Why don't you just say: . . ." and I'd give her the ending and she'd use it; one of them even rather immortal, talking about what a jackass I was . . . called "The Great Poet." an ambitious woman. they pop their cunts over you and their lips over your dick and expect all the answers.

Have written a hundred and ten poems in the last two weeks; a few of them are shit; 7 or 8 of them are immortal. [* * *]

[To John Martin]
August 2, 1974

Yes, that letter was from one of those modern sicks – thinks it's clever to steal a $35 or $15 book from the library and then write to the author and brag about it. hell, the best thing about a library book is that more than one person gets to read them (it).

And I'm to come by and eat dinner with him? Such an immense stupidity. Ow, ow, ow – and we're both poets! He says.

[To Carl Weissner]
November 7, 1974

Thanks the good letter. You over there in Germany waving Bukowski around feels damned fine to me. Glad you like *Burning*. It's been a long hot journey but I want to go on a long while yet ... typing ... and I hope the gods let me. Meanwhile my life is about the same — fighting the women, the horses; getting frightened and brave, up and down, low and high. [* * *]

Just in from Utah and Michigan. Michigan reading paid $500, plus air, plus room and food and booze. Cost 'em a grand to hear me sing. Stopped off in bookstore after reading. They'd advertised in the *Detroit Free Press*. 700 arrived, massed-in, asshole to asshole. I signed books, danced, read, drank and insulted people. It was crazy but I was so damned high I didn't care. Slept in hotel 200 years old, stayed 3 nights and days. Awakened one morning sick, retching, phoned down to switchboard lady: "Look, I have a complaint. I wake up sick here every morning and the first thing I've got to look at is that American flag out there. Can't something be done about it?" She got very pissyassed and asked if I didn't LIKE the American flag. "Look," I said, "I just told you. I'm sick and it makes me sicker. If that makes you uptight, just forget it's a flag. It's just a matter of white and red stripes waving in my face. And the stars. I've got a bad stomach." They didn't take the flag down for me, Carl.

Guy came over and got drunk with me last night. He wants to buy the movie options on *South of No North*. I drank his booze and then turned him over to Martin. The other guy just renewed his option on *Erections* and the guy who has *Post Office* says he has high hopes. If just one of these turns into a movie I'm going to buy a new pair of shoes.

Like you know: stay in the trenches and lob some out. I think we're wearing those sons of bitches out. ya.

[To the Editors of *The L.A. Free Press*]
November 15, 1974

Hello editors:

Regarding the Lynne Bronstein letter of Nov. 15 about my story of Nov. one:

1. The story was about pretentiousness in art. The fact that the pretender had female organs had nothing to do with the story in total. That any female made to look unfavorable in a story must be construed as a denunciation of the female as female is just so much guava. The right of the creator to depict characters any way he must remains inviolate – whether those characters are female, black, brown, Indian, Chicano, white, male, Communist, homosexual, Republican, peg-legged, mongolian and/or?

2. The story was a take-off on an interview with an established female poet in a recent issue of *Poetry Now*. Since I have been interviewed for a future issue of the same journal and for future editions of *Creem* and *Rolling Stone*, my detractors will get their chance to see how I hold or fail under similar conditions.

3. When the narrator lets us know that he has Janice Altrice's legs in mind might infer more that he is bored with the poetry game, and also might infer that he could have a poolhall, dirty joke mind, at times. That the narrator might be attacking himself instead of trying to relegate the lady back to a "sex object" evidently is beyond the belief of some so-called Liberated women. Whether we like it or not, sex and thoughts of sex do occur to many of us (male and female) at odd and unlikely times. I rather like it.

4. That "she is indeed speaking for Bukowski himself, who has expressed a similar contempt for unknown poets who give each other support." The lady spoke for herself. Her "contempt" was toward poets not academically trained. My dislike is toward all bad poetry and toward all bad poets who write it badly – which is most of them. I have always been disgusted with the falsity and dreariness not only of contemporary poetry but of the poetry of the centuries – and this feeling was with me before I got published, while I was attempting to get published, and it remains with me now even as I pay the rent with poesy. What kept me writing was not that I was so good but that that whole damned gang was so bad – when they had to be compared to the vitality and originality that was occurring in the other art forms. – As to those who must gather together to give each other support, I am one with Ibsen: "the strongest men are the most alone."

5. "Now that he's well-known and the only southern California poet published by Black Sparrow Press, he thinks that nobody else is entitled to be a poet – especially women." My dear lady: you are entitled to be whatever you can be; if you can leap twenty feet straight up into the air or sweep a 9 race card at the Western harness meet, please go ahead and do so.

6. "A lot of us think there's more to write poetry about than beer drunks, hemorrhoids, and how rotten the world is." I also think there's more to write poetry about than that and I do so.

7. "Female artists, on the other hand, try to be optimistic." The function of the artist is not to create optimism but to create art – which sometimes may be optimistic and sometimes can't be. The female is bred to be more optimistic than the male because of a function she has not entirely escaped as yet: the bearing of the child. After passing through pregnancy and child-birth, to call life a lie is much more difficult.

8. "Could it be that the male is 'washed-up' as an artist, that he has no more to say except in his jealousy, to spit on the young idealists and the newly freed voices of women?" Are these the thought concepts you come up with in your "ego-boosting" sessions? Perhaps you'd better take a night off.

9. "Poetry is an art form. Like all art forms, it is subjective and it does not have sex organs." I don't know about your poems, Lynne, but mine have cock and balls, eat chili peppers and walnuts, sing in the bathtub, cuss, fart, scream, stink, smell good, hate mosquitoes, ride taxicabs, have nightmares and love affairs, all that.

10. ". . . without being negative . . ." I thought they'd long ago ridden this horse to death; it's the oldest of the oldest hats. I first heard it around the English departments of L.A. high school in 1937. The inference, when you call somebody "negative," is that you completely remove them from the sphere because he or she has no basic understanding of life forces and meanings. I wouldn't be caught using that term while drunk on a bus to Shreveport.

11. I don't care for Longfellow or McKuen either, although they both possess (possessed) male organs. One of the best writers I knew of was Carson McCullers and she had a female name. If my girl friend's dog could write a good poem or a decent novel I'd be the first to congratulate the beast. That's Liberated.

12. Shit, I ought to get paid for this.

Charles Bukowski

[To A. D. Winans]
November [?], 1974

[★ ★ ★] About the foreword you yanked, o.k. That's what an editor's for . . . you either promulgate the thing or you reject it. In this game we all get stuff back, and sometimes get things taken and published that would have been better tossed away with the used condoms.

Been on the reading kick . . . the old survival suck . . . Detroit, Riverside, Santa Cruz . . . Ginsberg, Ferlinghetti, Snyder at S.C. Drew 1600 at 3 bucks a head. Benefit for Americans in Mexican jails . . . after the poets got their bit of cream. There was a bomb threat and old Allen's ears jumped. He got on stage and improvised a poem about the situation. Linda read too. Next day we hung around town testing the bars. They seemed to be a cut or two above the general slop pits of L.A.

Ginsberg was all right, he seemed a good sort. [★ ★ ★]

Haven't written too much while on this poetry reading tour. The juices are there; simply have to get into the habit of sitting at the Royal Altar . . . keeping letters short and staying away from the track . . . a bit . . . might be an aid.

Bukowski was now writing his novel Factotum.

[To John Martin]
December 4, 1974

Hard times are a-comin', kid. I hope we loop through. Let's get lucky against the tide. Why not? Meanwhile, these which I cracked out last night.

By the way, saw some of the work of this Tom Clark in *Poetry Now*. He really flows and gambles and plays it loose. I like his guts. Good, very, that you are publishing him. He's the raw gnawing end of the moon.

I know about the novel. Next envelope will prob. have a couple of chapters. I reread the fucking novel and get depressed; it doesn't quite have the spring and mox I wanted it to have. but as an easy whorehouse journal of madness I do think it scores. It's all the angle you want to look at it at. I think, though, the best thing to do is to finish it even if I finish it badly. Getting it published seems much more secondary.

[To Louise Webb]
December 23, 1974

It's about the same with me. Confusion, abject and candy-colored. Got Brahms on the radio . . . Thinking about Jon now. He gave me a powerful lift. He loved my shit. Those two books you guys did will never be topped. I look at them now and it's all so hard to believe. And now Jon's gone and the rare book dealers are raking in the green leaves. [* * *]

[To John Martin]
December 30, 1974

the screenplay shit was just some teacher wanting to do a student film. a) he doesn't seem to have the money. b) it's from *Erections* . . . a .45 to pay the rent . . . and Stone has the option on that. and c) he wants to come over and drink beer with me.

here's some poems. the novel will soon be done. I'll ship you 4 or 5 chapters in a few days. [* * *] If I don't get murdered I figure the novel will be finished by the end of January for better or worse. I don't think it's a great novel, but I think it's an odd one, a curious one and it reads easy. well, we'll see. did Hemingway talk like this? [* * *]

times are going to get deep hard and this machine is just going to have to toughen up. let's hope the Sparrow keeps flying. ah, I got a teaser for you. want to dedicate *Factotum* to John and Barbara Martin. now that's lard for the pan, isn't it?

• 1975 •

The documentary Bukowski *was made by Taylor Hackford and first shown in October 1973. See* Hank, *pp. 239–240.*

[To Carl Weissner]
February 19, 1975

[★ ★ ★] The documentary film on *Bukowski* just showed at Whitney museum along with one on Henry Miller and I'm told the *Bukowski* got a good write-up in the *New York Times*. I even get quite a few phone calls at night now from drunken young girls in Mississippi, Cincinnati, Philly and New York City. Those young girls just want to suck the soul out of a literary sort, right out of the top of his cock. I'm tougher on most of those calls than most would be, I'm sure. It feels good to send those chicks scattering back to their lead-weight boy friends.

The depression is here although the govt. prefers to call it a "recession." Which reminds me of the old one: a recession is when your friends are out of jobs, a depression is when you're out of one. It's at times like this that I'm glad I trained myself throughout a lifetime to detest a job of any sort. All these poor automobile workers sitting around glassy-eyed with homes half-paid for and cheating wives. They trusted that a hard day's work for a good day's pay would get them through. Now as the govt. tries to pump blood into the corpse they sit around and work crossword puzzles and look at daytime TV shows programmed to the female . . . the only thing that will cure this is the same thing that has cured every capitalistic depression since 1940 – another war; a big war, a little war, a hot war, a cold war, but war war war, and so we arm the Arabs and we arm the Jews and we send scout planes out once again in Vietnam, and I write my poems and drink my beer and try to get through the last 4 scenes in *Factotum*, and I fight with my girlfriend, hop a plane to Santa Barbara, pick up 300 bucks for making them laugh at Baudelaire, and I find myself on a house boat the next day with 3 crazy people and we're laughing at the ducks and the boats and the sky and everything we say, smoking that bad shit, and we're still alive and we walk down the docks later and all at once all the boat owners honk their horns at us and we wave our arms and wave our arms and the horns honk and honk all over the harbor, one picking it up after the other and not knowing why, and we wave our arms among all the honking, and as we get into the car and drive off they are still honking, you can hear them over the engine. You see, when I read in Santa Barbara, Carl, I even turn on the abalone fisherman and the mallards. somebody taped it with real professional equipment. it was a good crowd that night, drinking out of huge mugs of beer. if this guy spins me off a tape I should spin one off for you. charms.

[To Hank Malone]
April 20, 1975

I am still zonking on the poem and the story, no quitting, I guess. They're going to have to come get me, I can't do the Hemingway no matter how much I admired it. I guess I got started so late that I'm still trying to save ground.

Still trouble with the ladies; what a dirty, hard and relentless game that one can get to be.

Finished the 2nd novel. prob. out in Sept. it's a little rough and maybe a little corny but think it has some saving graces in the halfass mad desperateness of ye central charcoal.

uh huh.

your blithe and non-boring presence when I was in *Dee*troit not forgotten.

Winans published California Bicentennial Poets Anthology *in 1976.*

[To A. D. Winans]
April 29, 1975

got to say I'm glad you found some – so many – for the antho.

word leaking down here that you're getting drunk up there and kicking ass. the way I look at it, Frisco-wise, is that any ass you kick is the right one.

finished the 2nd novel. [★ ★ ★] it'll be a long time to do a third novel. if it ever comes it will probably have to do with the MAN-WOMAN situation, and that's a big bite out of the lurking dark. to do it well I'm going to have to grow up more, plenty more. may never grow that much. [★ ★ ★]

[To John Martin]
May 28, 1975

You must allow the writing to write itself. I can think of one in your particular stable who has simply written herself out by not waiting for the re-fill process. It's easy enough to do, this thing of getting very professional about your act. Ez did it, Ernie did it, and it didn't work, finally. You've been much more than an editor to me, and that's all right. But you have to trust my instincts. I make enough errors, that's part of it. But I think in the final addition the luck holds. Do you know what I mean? Sure you do. Relax.

p.s. – the drink won't get me. I know that monster too well. if I don't get murdered by a woman I'll burn up a hell of a lot more typer ribbons. yeh.

[To Mike – ?]
June 22, 1975

[★ ★ ★] maybe you're writing too much the way I write. I once wrote like William Saroyan for about 3 years until I decided that his content was candyass and only his rolling style had something to hang a hat to. so I took part of that. and part of Ernie and part of Celine and I had a little luck. maybe when you decide that I am candyass you'll have a better chance. [★ ★ ★]

Roth Wilkofsky was, with Karyl Klopp, editor of Pomegranate Press, North Cambridge, Massachusetts.

[To Roth Wilkofsky]
August 9, 1975

[* * *] Have had the flu and my balls actually ache and my girl friend is crying for sex sex sex, and yes I've heard the Bruckners you mention but I don't have a phono, but always glad when I get Bruck, by luck, on the radio. He's good sound listening, puts it right on the rail. I think he's terribly under-estimated because he sucked to Wagner so much, but unlike his master he didn't fuck his work up so much with the human voice, which is most of the time one of the worst sounding instruments. yah. [* * *]

[To Carl Weissner]
August 28, 1975

[* * *] there's too much to do here too — meaning writing, drinking, fights with women, drinking, playing the horses, drinking, fights with women, drinking, and visits by people who do me very little good. I'm going to have to get harder with the door knockers. there have become so many of them. each thinking that they are the *special* ones, that they have something to say, something for me to *drink*, something for me to listen to. some of them even have balls enough to bring their WRITING. kindness sometimes only begets pain. these people have nothing but time to lounge around in. I don't mind wasting time as long as I do it in *my* way, it's somehow still not so bad. but after they drip their tiny souls all over me it's a long time getting back to where I can even feel less than half-sick. 99 per cent of the world consists of bloodsuckers who must feed and feed and feed. I am going to send them to another bucket of blood. [* * *]

The Russian composer's full name is Reinhold Moritzovich Glière.

[To Roth Wilkofsky]
September 4, 1975

[★ ★ ★] 3:30 p.m. on my 2nd beer. rolling Prince Albert. something on the radio. what is it? I've heard it, yes. many times. can't spell it. Illeia Morovitz by Gliere? long strains and strands.

have in mind to shape up a few of the ten or 12 poems I wrote last night. when drinking one tends to use too many lines but a certain gamble comes about and you use some lines you'd probably never use when you're sober. mostly I hack out the flowers and leave in the brambles.

Bruckner and Mahler, yes. I could never quite get it on with the Bee. Don't know why. Bach was easy because he didn't have to carry around a lot of excess crap. anyhow, classical music and booze – taken together – have carried me through many a night when it seemed as if there were nothing else around. and maybe there wasn't.

[To John Martin]
September 19, 1975

Oh, John – meant to get these straight and to you earlier – one night's work – but I've been fighting off these sex-mad teeny-boppers. can you use a half dozen? Barbara need never know.

Charles Plymell is the author of many books of poems from various small presses.

[To Charles Plymell]
October 29, 1975

[★ ★ ★] My ass is really strapped for time but I burn and slobber away a lot of time anyhow, and have been meaning to answer your letter which I appreciated . . . *Rolling Stone* Mag by today shooting photos for an article on Bukowski which they say should appear in the next issue or two. The cover of *Time* mag is next and then I will end up sucking my own dick with my legs strapped around the bedposts.

The whole problem is how serious a man can take what the media does to and/or for him. What one should realize is that the media puffs up a hell of a lot of stale fruitcake ... like Joe Namath, Bob Hope, Robert Ford, Henry Ford, Zippo Marx, dead Kenny's x-wife widow, all that. Most creative artists are weak because they are emotional, and because it's hard and dirty work even though it's most interesting work. They fall to exposure, camera flashes, that grisly attention. I think that when any creative artist gets good enough society has an Animal out There that the artist is fed to so he won't get any stronger. Creativity, no matter what you say, is somehow bound up with adversity, and when you get dangerous enough they simply take away your adversity. They've done it with the blacks, they've done it with the Chicanos, they've done it with the women, and now they're playing with me. I intend to allow them to clutch a loud, empty fart for their reward. I will be elsewhere, cleaning my toenails or reading the *Racing Form*.[1] [★ ★ ★]

[To Charles Plymell]
December 3, 1975

[★ ★ ★] I am riven. Female claw of ballsoul. Yet when one figures one is rifted and lost forever ... there are more knocks upon the door, and here each one enters more beautiful than the one lost. I mean, what rivening shit, eh, Chaz? What I am trying to say is that I hurt in the proper places and I move very slowly toward a new person ... but miracle flowers arrive and perch themselves upon me. It's as if they know that I need help. I love them, their cunthairs and my tongue dribbling in between. At my age, I ought to be playing checkers at the corner park. I'm drunk, yes. Reading in New York City, the Bowery bit, June 23, they tell me. I might round out in Baltimore ... only payment I'd need would be a couple of young cunts I could eat out alive. No siffed-up shit, bastard. I've never had v.d. Just something that looks good and would might maybe diminish the minor tremblings of a tottering soul, hey hey hey ...

---

1. Cp. "The artist, like the God of the creation, remains within or behind or beyond or above his handiwork, invisible, refined out of existence, indifferent, paring his fingernails." – *A Portrait of the Artist as a Young Man*.

Black Sparrow Press moved from Los Angeles to Santa Barbara in the fall of 1975.

[To John Martin]
December 3, 1975

now that you've moved I realize how tremendous our relationship has been. anyhow, if you've got the guts to cot down in a different area and continue, I imagine I might have too. tra lala.

Linda problem sloved . . . solved . . . I've been drinking. miscarriage. so we can still shoot for that 50 grand death pact. [★ ★ ★]

lost and lousy and lovely girls coming by almost each night. what shit. do you think they'd do this for a postal clerk? (by the way, I keep the hard-earned bankroll *intact*.) [★ ★ ★]

The novel mentioned in the following is Factotum, *which was officially published on December 18, 1975.*

[To John Martin]
December 10, 1975

Well, here's the new machine – $143.10, tax included. I was out one night and came home and Linda had broken in. All my books were gone, plus the typer, radio, paintings and various items. Linda was crouched behind a brush and started smashing things when she saw me, and screaming. Some of the things, items have simply vanished, others demolished, including the typer which she bounced against the street again and again. She also broke my windows, so forth. I am putting things back together and trying to start over again. I am in semi-state of shock so please don't expect too much literary work until after Xmas. o.k.?

Like you know, I am really waiting on the novel. As soon as it comes out please AIRMAIL me a copy . . .!

Just wanted to get this thing off to let you know circumstances. I've puttied back in all the windows and it's quiet tonight. I intend to go on. There's novel #3 you know, and more p o e m s and D I R T Y stories, and I hope you're settled and all's in order, and hello to Barbara.

[To John Martin]
December 14, 1975

things are very nice right now, and it's damn well time they should be. the health, the feelings, the flow is (are) still in good running order. my pre-training holds me in ultra good stead. carry on, rally forth, all that. shit, it's only the 8th round and I've got a good cornerman to patch up the cuts. rah rah rah. or have I finally gone nuts?

stead? is there such a word?

I would be the last one to slap you with a merry Xmas. I'd rather wish you lucky midnights and more submissive and obedient shipping clerks – than the next to last.

you tell Barbara that I'm going to answer the motherfucking bell for the 9th round.

• 1976 •

[To John Martin]
January 6, 1976

here's more poems.

I'm still thinking in terms of starting the 3rd novel in a couple of months. I'm not quite sure I'm man enough to handle it. You know, tones of vindictiveness, all that. Unless the slant and the laughter and the judgement get off of beggary it's almost a waste. The problem is not so much what I feel but what everybody must feel in similar traps. Tra lala. [★ ★ ★]

The new novel announced here as Love Tales of the Hyena *eventually was published as* Women *in December, 1978.*

[To John Martin]
January 22, 1976

[★ ★ ★] Have you ever read Catullus? There's a translation by Carl Sesar via Mason & Lipscomb, seems full of butter, fire and laughter. Too bad Cat seemed to have drifted off into homosexuality. That may be a standard literary trait but it always discourages me. Anyhow, he could lay down a line, and he was dead around the age of 30. Them there war the daze; it seems like slavery creates art. can you send me a couple of slaves, John? virginal, about 15 with golden sensitive hairs about the boxes? I wait . . .

my Boswell – Pleasants – says he has discovered some typos in *Facto*. [★ ★ ★] I've heard some good sounds from people who've read the book. But get ready for critical attacks. If you can take it, I can write some more. Title for 3rd novel *Love Tales of the Hyena*. I've written a chapter out of the center. But whether I ever write the thing or how long it takes, that's drizzle out of a long spread from nowhere.

Hey, you tell Barbara that the book design was super superbia exellente. . . . DON'T FORGET! [★ ★ ★]

[To John Martin]
January 24, 1976

Thanks for the good words in ye Calendar section of ye good ol' *L.A. Times*.

If the game ends right here it has very well been worth it, that big run right up through center banging against malarkey and piss-ants, tradition, whores, fags, schools, sharks.

I'm still at Hollywood and Western, there's a potato boiling behind me, the health is amazingly good and it's very quiet here tonight. I could go to the phone and get trouble but I think I'll just let things lay easy.

Did you see the Foreman-Lytle fight on tv? What a ball-busting back-alley drunkeroo. Well, it wasn't dull but if that's what championship contenders are made of Ali is going to be around like a Bukowski sucking a beerbottle. For a long time.

[To Katherine – ?]
January 25, 1976

you are like sunlight
sunlight walking around.

you don't know how good
you are.
you play with my seriousness,
make me laugh.

when you comb your hair
all the gods come down
from the mountain
and watch

you are the woman
all women should have
been.

I ache with disbelief and
yearning

no matter how you turn
your body
or what you say
it is the perfect diamond
the perfect cut
the perfect glow

and when you get the blues
I get the blues
because I don't want you
to get the blues

in my life
I've told two other
women that I loved
them

I wouldn't say it to
you

one of those women
died
and another died
in another way
if I never see you again
I will always carry you
inside
outside

on my fingertips
and at brain edges

and in centers
centers
centers
of what I am of
what remains.

[To Carl Weissner]
February 13, 1976

Kaput in Hollywood, I really like that title – you're making me look good. Hope Martin goes your book of projected Buk poem translations. But I'm hot on *Factotum*, my last novel. Ya seen it yet? I think it's the best writing I've done. have gotten quite a bit of mail about it agreeing with me. In fact, today I got a letter with return address of Henry Miller, Pacific Palisades, and I thought, my my, is the old man bending to write me? But when I opened it up it was from his son, one Larry Miller. Ah well. He praised *Factotum*, part of which goes: "... I guess I just wanted to say thank you for being the first writer since reading my father that has made me feel that all is not lost in literature today; especially a sense of reality that seems to have escaped nearly everyone else . . ."

Oh, Cupcakes . . . she's got it. Miss Pussycat of 1973, she's 23, brains, body, spirit . . . Flaming red hair, long . . . she's in front of my bedroom mirror now combing that flame as I type this to you. she'll be the death of me, but it's worth it, pal. [* * *]

I'm going to swing around and read in Pittsburgh, Boston, New York City. Big time, Buk. looking out of superjet windows, looking at stewardesses' asses wiggling, ordering drink after drink . . . in there with the businessmen and swindlers and killers. I'm finally where I belong, Carl: the poetry-kill: I'll fuck 'em in the left ear with a distorted sonnet. . . .

[To John Martin]
March 28, 1976

[* * *] one of my problems is with Scarlet . . . Cupcakes . . . we've rifted. she's a speed-freak, pill-head and on the smack. you just don't know how HARD people can get until you've met one of those. and, of course, I got sucked-in early. you've seen the poems. John, will I ever meet a woman who is good to me? I suppose a lot of my problem is EGO, and at 55 I should be laying down that game altogether. as long as I've lived I'm just too fucking soft inside. but, baby, don't worry, we'll pull through this one just like we pulled through the others. not because we don't care but because we do.

the plans now are for my first vacation. I should be in Austin April 8th to meet Katherine and stay with her a couple of weeks. that is if Linda doesn't arrive and kill me first. I've been hearing quite a bit from her via phone and mail and she seems to be making overtures. I think I should kool it with her, tho. she's simply crazy. then there's another in Texas, Suzzana. Suzzana has a load of money, wants to marry me, take me to Paris, all that shit. do you think I could write a poem in Paris, big John? advise.

meanwhile, I hope to keep going on *Hyena*. if I can write that one, B.J., people will forever stop talking about *The Ginger Man*. there are so many unbelievable layers of laughter and love and blood madness ensconced there . . . you just don't know what's been happening to this old man while he's been sending you these tiny poems.

Katherine is the kindest one I've known. but you know how a writer is – he'll go for the sloppiest whore and the meanest bitch on earth – hoping to cure it or understand it or at least live with it . . . temporarily. [* * *] even tho I can't spell I think my writing is getting better and better. I can feel all those words inside of me, puffing and blowing, and it doesn't even scare me to talk about it. I'm loaded to the ear lobes. both ways.

These are from a series of mostly undated, mostly holograph notes, addressed sometimes to "Pam," "Scarlet," "Cupcakes," or "Cups," a woman who lived in the same apartment complex as Bukowski. The parenthetical date of the first one is noted on the manuscript and initialled "P.B."

[To Pamela Brandes]
[mid-1976]

Tues. night Wednesday morning [April 6, 1976]
 Pam, Pam, Pam, where are you? I love you. I love you. I love you.

§

3:45 A.M., Monday
 I *love* you, you bitch. I'll be gone for a *month*. I only wanted to *look* at you and say *goodbye*.

§

1:30 A.M. Sunday morning
 Red death sunset blood glory gal –
 Why is it that you are the one woman I have met who has not loved me entirely, madly and out of context? It confuses me. You must be my superior. Well, that's all right. – I mean, if I can win 8 races out of 9 I can expect to be upset by a longshot.
 [★ ★ ★]
[*signed "blubberboy Charley" with a drawing and arrow pointing to "Tears of Agony" dropping from the figure's eyes*]

§

June 5, 1976
 Cupcakes:
 you've made me write a lot of poems. (another enclosed). some of the poems are nasty and vindictive, some of them are lousy, but some of them are good, so I've got to thank you, gal. I hope that we can remain friends . . . in spite of some of our rough spots. keep it together.

§

Pam:
> I HATE YOU FOR NOT ADMITTING YOU LOVE ME.
> you are acting like a stupid cunt.

you will only suffer and suffer and suffer because there is a difference in what you feel and what SOCIETY wants you to feel.

the best way to anywhere is the most honest and truest way.

you've been fighting it.

you say you want to be a writer.

begin at the beginning.

your friend, Hank

§

Saturday, 1 p.m.

I miss you little Reds. Come see me soon.

§

Pam –

I'm sorry I got mad. But I give you money, your mother money, buy booze and cigarettes and dope and you treat me like a dog. I mean, hell, look at my viewpoint once in a while. Even though I may be unrealistic.

p.s. – your mother phoned. I suppose she's found you by now. keep yourself together. I still *like* you a lot.

§

Scarlet:

Come on down and see me sometimes. I've got some more Southern Comfort for your strep. I even won at the track – no horseshit. Well, keep it together.

Hollywood Hank

§

My dear Pamela Brandes:

You *too* can be replaced.

Hank

§

Pam –

I didn't mean it. I still love you. It's just that you never show any feeling toward me, and Jesus Christ that sometimes cuts in pretty deep.

I don't mean to load myself on you. I'll work it out. It's just going to take me a bit of time to figure out what the hell's happening.

Hank

§

7–1–76

Pam –

Thanks a hell of a lot of shit for nothing.

[To John Martin]
May 3, 1976

enclosed some poems.

I have gone a bit mad, and there's a reason. Anyway, I will be flitting about the country most of May, and June I'll go back to work except for the N.Y.C. reading. [★ ★ ★]

I have to get out of this court for a while. Things are very hard and ugly here right now. I feel that by the time I get back that she (Scarlet) will be moved out from this place in the back.

I'll be all right. No Dylan Thomas coming up. I am in more danger of doing it right here – looking up with her window light shining down from above in back, or no light for a couple of nights. I am hooked upon her barbarity – ruthless and raw – but know it's a shit trap and must work my way out.

[To John Martin]
June 7, 1976

don't worry; nobody's going to crawl into bed with me unless she almost deserves it. about the *Rolling Stone* interview – that's just another test the mother gods are laying upon me. I ain't going to wilt to the sound of late trumpets semi-heralding a late and minor fame. please don't worry about me, boss, I am too crazy to go crazy.

about Cups – she's got a hook into me and she knows it – but she's gone too, and talks to me straight, she promises nothing. and that's a better game than any I know that's GOING around. I've been drinking. so some of the CAPITALIZATION is accidental.

about the novel — I can't take guidance or I'm fucked. I mean, let me write it choppy. that's not all accidental. novels put me to sleep because they are not choppy. when we lose the raw sloppy gambling edge, then we are truly finished — turkeys. see the Dos Passos trilogy *USA*. I enjoyed his attempt — the idea was there — but he chopped it too fine. There is a difference between a 2 year old kid beating upon the back of a saucepan with a spoon and symphony, say, by — anybody. I have the feeling that the secret or the glow or the luck is somewhere in between. what I'm trying to say here is that I'm not writing *Hyena* for the *Free Press*. it comes out like it comes out, and I'm sorry I have but only one death to give to Bukowski. I'll probably rewrite the fucking thing, anyhow, when I get the full scan of it written I can mend parts, throw out parts, glue parts, add parts. but it's fairly close to home now, I feel it more than I can see it. but let me wobble through the first course, then maybe I will be able to see my balls from my cerebellum. [* * *]

[To A. D. Winans]
June 7, 1976

[* * *] I did one reading for a grand. I ask $500 plus air and plus . . . for others. keeps me at home. where I belong instead of waking up in bed with a teacher of retarded children in Tallahassee, Fla. and waking up in another bed with another teacher of retarded children in T. Fla. the next morning, no toilet paper in her crapper, I gotta write [*sic*] off my shitty bung with a brown paper bag into a beershit that will not let go. this ever happened to Ezra? [* * *]

I am in trouble with women as usual. they are getting younger and more vicious and more beautiful. they are my superiors. they kill me, almost. [* * *]

[To Carl Weissner]
July 13, 1976

[* * *] as usual, the women have me on the old cross. I am sitting around waiting for Cupcakes O'Brien's footsteps. Her shoes, hairpins, mirrors, stockings, underwear, lotions everywhere . . . but where is *she*? Cups, you bitch, appear!

Off to Columbus, Ohio, tomorrow . . . The *Hustler* magazine flying me out round trip, putting me into a hotel to interview me the next day. I feel like Hemingway. I hope they hustle me up a nice piece of ass. They've bought a couple of short stories from me . . . they *say over the phone* . . . I await the solid feel of a *check*, however. Columbus, Ohio, that's where Thurber came from, you know. I will shake his invisible hand when I land at the airport.

you keep close touch, old buddy. we are just beginning to blast the shit out of their bungholes! the women won't kill us, the booze won't kill us, the smog and the horses won't kill us, God won't kill us and the devil isn't interested. our journey through this . . . will be remembered. I am drinking steam beer, fan on my ass, good music on the radio; the sky is turning red and the dead sit on their palms just as they were meant to do.

[To A. D. Winans]
July 13, 1976

Have meant to answer sooner but I've been on the road. now going again – to Columbus, Ohio, Thurber's x-hangout.

as per a quote for back of your book, could you use this one?:

> A. D. Winans is one of the few writers I have met
> (and I've met too god damned many of them) who
> doesn't *act* like a writer or think of himself
> continually as a *writer*, and maybe that's why he
> writes better than they do. I always prefer a man I can
> tolerate for more than ten minutes – that's rare, and
> so is A. D.
> – Charles Bukowski

[* * *] down here with women I am having much trouble. I am over-emotional, not wordly, and my feelings get hooked in when others might be playing games. I get burned, pal, but it has almost always been that way. [* * *]

can you give me any advice on women, kid? they are waving my guts on the ends of their flagsticks.

[To John Martin]
September 13, 1976

[* * *] on the novel, *Love Tale of the Hyena*, I may have to wait a while. I think my nose might be too close to the mirror at the moment. there's no use writing a bad novel early when you might write a better one later. there are holy mathematical equations running through my mind – ha, ha – and I might take the woman and mix her into 3 women. Uh, I just don't know. I play around with these things in my head – when? – I don't know. But maybe we'd better delay things and do them more or less right – right meaning the taste and the flow of a good thing. I feel that this novel just didn't start with the right . . . easiness of laughter and terror. we're just going to have to wait, baby, and it may never arrive but that's better than having it arrive asshole badly and as journalese . . . or however the shit it dies. [* * *]

[To A. D. Winans]
September 13, 1976

[* * *] Things are still shitty here, I mean spiritually shitty. The redhead I was in love with for a while, the former part-time hooker told me today she has gone back to it. She did a trick last night for $100. I cashed the motherfucker's check for her. It will probably bounce. [* * *]

I am luckier than most; I have various other sources of fulfillment – female, of course. But I doubt that there is any real woman upon the horizon (for me, my mind, my need, my weakness) and I'll probably go to my death without ever seeing her – which hardly makes my life any different from another man's. Yet I keep feeling that she's out there, somewhere, but how do you get to her?

Christ, what a lack of grace, what a shit-smeared moon, night, day, noon, 3:45 p.m. [★ ★ ★]

[To Carl Weissner]
October 16, 1976

[★ ★ ★] Cupcakes and I are finished. I have 3 new girlfriends but she can't seem to be replaced – none so vicious, so evil, she was a real witch with long red hair. It's going to take me a long time to get over this one. I was thinking of coming to Germany with her but now that it's over I don't want to come. [★ ★ ★]

I can't write much more. I am sitting here with this spear stuck into my gut that Cupcakes jammed into me. pure pure blithering agony.

you hold and I'll try to hold.

[To A. D. Winans]
October 26, 1976

[★ ★ ★] I am still mending from the Cupcakes disaster; it's a slow heal . . . the eternal beautiful witch-factor. she is killing off some other poor sucker soul as I write this. some people need to kill, it's an instinct, it keeps their neon juices flowing.

Do you think you'll ever be able to give up editing? It's my suggestion that you do . . . before the dogs eat off your toes.

Get out, Al, and take a plane and go lay down next to J. W. for a week. eat breakfast together and get drunk at night. there aren't any poets; gather real valuables. get the hell out of North Beach and go East of no West.

and allah be wit de.

[To John Martin]
October 27, 1976

[* * *] not to hex myself, but anyhow I think after Nov. 13 I'll jump into this novel I have in mind: *Women*. whether it works or not.

I don't think I'll ever be able to do the childhood bit. oyee, maybe when I'm 70 but you know some woman is going to kill me before I reach 60.

[To John Martin]
November 2, 1976

oh, I ain't quite quit yet. I feel I'm in a slump, swinging at the outside curve out of the strike zone. the redhead still bites me inside my gut even though I know she is a deathly scorpion bringdown . . . so I'm rather batting .143 in the minors. I get to pinch hit now and then, I hope to get the swing back. I feel I still have it. it just has to rise up to meet me.

meanwhile, the checks look great, I hope the sales hold. I wouldn't feel good if you sent me money that didn't come from royalty sources. I'm not your son. hardly. and if things narrow down you cut the margin down. the bankroll looks *good* . . . I've had to open another account next door at the Bank of America. oh, christ. what I mean is that I don't have the needs of most people and I live cheaply. this will help me keep writing. I'd rather not be a janitor in my last years. so I'm careful with my money, even though the redhead took me for about $500. a real artist, she. [* * *]

[To A. D. Winans]
November 2, 1976

[* * *] yes, watch those young girls, Al. their sincerity seems so sincere until they don't get what they really wanted, then they move on in the hunt. meanwhile we get burnt down believing that they wanted *us*. we let our egos waylay us, it's so easy. then the truth comes up and we can't believe what was obviously the believable.

on short stories, I think the best idea is to write them the way you want to write them, then look for a market. the deliberate slant automatically takes the juice out.

keep it together.

[To A. D. Winans]
November 30, 1976

My spiritual advisors have told me not to give any more mixed readings. — but no shit, they are a bringdown. I like Alta, you and Miche[line] but it just won't work. it causes a scratching I don't like. so I've got to say more. like: no. call me a shit but there's a lot of shit in the river.

Miche has never got his just due but it's as well — it'll keep him on his spring instead of turning him into a silky-haired, over-read, over-precious N. Mailer. overexposure is the toughest whore of all. and one that few men can turn away for a head job.

you're right on the women. they can eat your time, they can eat you out. but, finally, they will leave you alone for a while — they make master moves on the chessboards of cunt-cock steel-wall play. but what material. I realize that I have gotten locked almost into this area. but that too will pass. and then I can write about the cockroaches, or whatever is left. [★ ★ ★]

I miss that belly dancer. We laughed for almost 9 days and nights. she said I caused the laughter but it was her, she made me feel so good and crazy. Sometimes there's luck. When there is you stock up on it and wait for the other times. [★ ★ ★]

• 1977 •

[To John Martin]
January 8, 1977

everything's lovely except there's a madwoman on my bed and her back faces mine and she has covered herself with a blanket. I really draw them. she's been like that for an hour. I doubt I'll ever die a natural death. o, poems enclosed. keep it up. mine is.

[To John Martin]
January 10, 1977

I've got a reading on the 30th of this month, which means poems, so I'm going to hang with the poem until then, hoping for new juices and so forth. Then in Feb. we start the 3rd novel, *Women*. I mean, I'll start it. And if it doesn't roll by itself I'll just stop. Let me be the judge. and jury. and the killer. ah.

anyhow, I'm glad you're on a new book of poems. 1976 was one of my roughest years. since I was in my early 20's. so much happened and so much failed. It was like I had to learn all over again, and that's good. those big eyes looking into one's soul aren't always telling the truth no more than the roses are or the fish are or the mountains are. [* * *]

[To Hank Malone]
January 16, 1977

Lost your address, found it. Have also been going through a bit of rough time via some trollop-strumpet red haired witch. One is not too interested in literary essays when one is walking around with a knife in the gut. It's still there. But – as in your essay – one goes on. Wow. Endurance is more important than truth, I says.

Hank, the essay hits some points pretty good – the alcohol bit-need, the carry-on in face of constant shellfire, and the need – sometimes – for laughter. Sometimes instead of dying or killing myself I just go to bed for a couple of days. Shades down, swilling in the swill.

There are always more women but the one that's wanted and the one that's gotten a bit is the one that works you over good. And never leaves you alone long enough to get over the trap.

You got any advice for me on women – send right off.

Me, I'm watching James Cagney. *White Heat*. and drinking white wine. thanks for mailing me the essay.

[To Carl Weissner]
January 27, 1977

[* * *] the mailman found me passed out in bed, hungover, at 2 p.m. in the afternoon. "Charley," he said, "I got you a little letter here." he's o.k. he sees me with young girls, hags, and I'm usually drunk or drinking. got a couch outside. 2 young German girls came to see me one day. I tried to fuck both of them, finally settled on the older (22) and the other went for a long walk, and maybe it was limp dick but it seemed she had a corkscrew pussy. sometimes there are those and they work good. I say, "ah, ah, look I'm sliding way up around the left side but I'm in, somehow I'm in, I'm no boy scout, I'm in, and ah ah ah . . ." but maybe I wasn't in *this* one. I kept punching at a tunnel-ending. I gave off and ate her out. they stayed for 3 or 4 days and nights until I got tired. then I drove them off to some woman's place in the hills and I drank cans of beer steering out of there, and little cans of vodka mix, red or pink cans, the sunlight blaring in at me, wondering if I were nuts or the world has calmed, but really nothing much, I found my way back in, stretched it out, went to sleep for a couple of hours, the phone rang . . . [* * *]

This is the first mention in these letters of Linda Lee Beighle whom Bukowski eventually married on August 18, 1985.

[To Carl Weissner]
March 3, 1977

[★ ★ ★] have heard from Ferling.'s bookkeeper. I think his overseas cut is 50 percent. it can't be helped. but it does leave a goodly sum. John Martin is nicer. His cut is ten percent and so far he has always been good enough to waive it.

Cupcakes has vanished into space. not really. she's after the gold fillings and after a young dentist who plays with them. smart girl. got some new ladies, a little less related to the shark. Linda Lee – the # one new one (not Linda King – x) studying German. she thinks we're going to Germany. well, who the hell knows? [★ ★ ★]

[To A. D. Winans]
Late April, 1977

Thanks for sending your special issue to the Germans. Things are working up over there – 4 or 5 of my books in translation. I think the Germans have me down as an admixture of Bogart, Hem, Adolf, and Jack the Ripper. I may go there this summer with my lady friend. Drink and die there. The Fatherland. [★ ★ ★]

[To John Martin]
May 10, 1977

Enclosed the bit from Germany. It's nice that you take 10 per cent instead of 50 like Mr. Lawrence F. He wrote me the other day suggesting that City Lights put out a Bukowski "selected poems." I haven't answered. I've told him time and again that I am in the Sparrow's nest.

The Germans are honest and I think Carl W. keeps them that way.

On the other hand there is *London Mag* who put out *Post Office* and *Life and Death in a Charity Ward* and not a sound, not an advance, no royalties. These books were issued in 1974. I wrote the editor inquiring about the matter about a year and a half ago. No response.

Well, it's just like the women – the writing's still the thing. No matter what they do or don't do to you. [* * *]

[To Carl Weissner]
May 11, 1977

[* * *] although I no longer live on one candy bar a day, life still kicks my ass pretty hard, mostly in the form of people, mostly in the form of women, a real crazy rip. sometimes very authentic and horrifying, so you see the gods are still playing with me. don't worry, old friend, if some woman doesn't kill me there is a lot more coming via the word.

Martin phones: "Weissner is the one responsible for getting you over in Germany. He is a very good man."

"Hell, I *know* it," I say, "and he even collects my bills for me. And I have the *strange* feeling that the son of a bitch *improves* my writing when he translates it."

I talk to my present girlfriend Linda Lee about you. "I've got to do something for Carl. Maybe I should send him some money."

"No," she says, "do something really nice for him."

"Like what?" I say. It's hard, Carl, for me to do something nice. I'm going to dedicate a book to you some day, hurrah. but that don't buy no groceries. well, anyhow, thanks for all the damned work you've done. thanks again. Jesus christ, yes. [* * *]

my 89 year old uncle is alive in Andernach. Heinrich Fett. and, did I tell you? – the house I was born in still stands but is now a brothel. I can get the address from my biographer if you want to get a piece of ass in the house that Buk was born in. [* * *]

[To Hank Malone]
May 27, 1977

Yes, I read your piece again – the altered one – and you know it's difficult for me to say whatever. You must know that I don't know who I am or why I do what I do, and that if I did know I probably couldn't do whatever I am doing now.

I don't ask you to feel guilty in choosing me as subject matter but don't ask me to feel guilty either, or to understand anything about it. You must know this. You must know that I'm unable to handle it – not out of modesty but simply out of whatever makes me functional.

I have no feelings about most writing – past or present – except that I dislike most of it, can't read it.

Thanks, anyhow, for sending this on. [* * *]

[To Carl Weissner]
August [?17], 1977

[* * *] I don't care much for the record *90 Minutes in Hell*. The title wasn't my idea. and I don't care for most of it, except for the short story that ends it. I think I did a good job there.

There seems to be plenty of people knocking on my door nowadays and they just seem to sit and sit and sit, and it's like they are crunching on the hours and I am the only one who seems to feel it. they can't take hints. finally, after much agony I politely inform them that I'd like to do a little work. you can't tell them you want to take a shit because they'll wait that out.

Went down to Del Mar with Linda Lee and we got stinko in our motel room and went swimming and diving in the rough surf at 1:30 a.m. A real gasser and not a bad way to die but I came on out and we got back to the motel, poured some more, and got along that night. She's a good girl and has lived through many of my drunken, mad, unkind nights and has forgiven me . . . so far.

[To Carl Weissner]
September 22, 1977

[* * *] Got first copy of *Love Is a Dog from Hell* in mail yesterday. Finished the novel *Women* last night: 433 pages, 99 chapters. I think it's all right but it will confuse some people; others will simply hate me, as usual. They may even put a hit man on me? [* * *]

Now it's back to the short story and the poem again.

That novel was a real juicer for me (*Women*). I mean it *gave* me energy, it didn't take it from me. I feel strangely lost now . . .

All the Germans who come by drink Coors which is one of the worst beers in America. I can't sip it without puking. [* * *]

[To John Martin]
October 9, 1977

[* * *] I sent the corrected pages of the novel off a couple of days ago. It still read o.k. to me. had to make another name change – from Ruthie to Cecelia. The woman was Ruthie Wantling and I thought that was getting too close.

[To John Martin]
October 17, 1977

[* * *] word from Carl: the blue book has gone into 53,000 copies. word from publisher: by the end of the year they will have 70,000 copies out. to me, those are astonishing figures, and so much of it is due to Weissner, his translation of the works and his getting it in front of people.

I write things because it is some kind of disease but once that's over I think it's all right if some other people get caught on the same sickness, you know? [* * *]

[To A. D. Winans]
October 27, 1977

you sound down. it's probably all those big mouths down there – up there – proclaiming their greatness. the longer I know of the poets the more sick I believe they really are – asking for decency and love and understanding from the world in their poems and, in person, being exactly the opposite of what they ask for. there's a speech for you. ah.

things here are fairly quiet. have more or less settled with a good woman, Linda Lee, after running through quite a number. getting fucked by many is not so important; it's a settling for an easy clarity that I think helps the nights, the days, the months. [* * *]

[To A. D. Winans]
November 2, 1977

[* * *] get on the white wine, A. D. beer is fattening, the hard stuff eats the gut, the liver, and it's hard to type under the hard stuff. good white wine, German, can be had for around 3.50 a bottle. 2 bottles of this can make a nice evening and you won't wake up feeling like you've been swallowing wet cat turds all night. also, before you start to drink take a tablespoonful of metamucil or one of maalox. if all this sounds chickenshit to you or rails against the spirit, don't do it. the way I see it, I'm 57 and I've proved I can drink as long and as hard as the next. I think the time comes when the long-ignored body asks for a bit of kindness. it has waited around a long time on the doorstep . . .

the poets? well, I prefer the fishermen and the corner newsboys. I don't know where people ever got the idea that poets and poetry was (is) the holy thing. I think the only time poetry gets any good is when it forgets its holiness, and that's very seldom. take Ezra Pound – Pound as good as he was with the language he made that place a temple and a sanctuary. any man down on skid row would have preferred a can of beans. I'm not saying the poet owes anything to the masses; I find the masses both disgusting and interesting. it still might be good if they found us the same way? Whitman said that to have great poetry we must have great audiences. I think he had it backwards.

yes, Linda Lee is a good woman. I was due for some luck. she is a stayer with a gentle courage and doesn't play man against man as if she were some golden cow. I've had some bad ones, many bad ones. the percentages have come around and I am able to accept them. [★ ★ ★]

Martin says *Women* out in June. o.k. you're going to know many of the people in this one, I may get killed for this one. it's written as some type of high-low comedy and I look worse than anybody but they're only going to think about how I painted *them*. it's a jolly roaring blast, I think, and when I re-read it I realize that I must have been crazy from 1970 to 1977. like Thomas Wolfe, after this one, I can't go home again. it was quite easy to write and it didn't take too much guts on 3 bottles of white wine a night. oh, ah, oh . . .

Martin has been good to me, I am one of the few wild cards in his deck. If your stuff comes back, realize that he sticks fairly close to poetry as craft, the well-honed line, rather like voices speaking out from behind wallpaper, the sublime traditionalism: Douglas Woolf, Reznikoff, Eshleman, Corman, Creeley, Loewinsohn.

For my money, Micheline, Richmond, Winans are closer to the blood-source, but then I'm not an editor or a publisher, and Martin has been good to me, he picked me up early and gave me a chance to get out of the post office when nobody else was listening. I can't forget this and I won't. he's my publisher. I've got the hound-dog loyalty and I don't mind; it feels good. but it is hard for me to read or agree with who he *does* print. all right, I type on. [★ ★ ★]

[To A. D. Winans]
November 9, 1977

[★ ★ ★] yes, I'm down to one woman now. after re-reading *Women* I decided I needed a rest. some aren't going to believe that novel. I can't blame them, but there's very little fiction to it.

you seem to know a lot of women who have passed into the vapor. I mean death. Linda King phoned from Arizona not too long ago. She claims she's now a lush & she's pregnant. she sounded quite sad. she gave me a hard row. after we split I met two other women named Linda. I meet a lot of Lindas and lot of Joans and Joannas – mostly names that end in "a". it's curious. [★ ★ ★]

[To A. D. Winans]
November 13, 1977

Could you tear up the poem "a very serious fellow"? I don't think Steve [Richmond] could handle it. there are many reasons why I don't think he can handle it but don't want to number them here. just *trust* me and rip up the poem. I am asking Martin to destroy the same. I think the poem is accurate but I knew Steve pretty well personally and I just don't want to have him go under the damage . . .

o.k.?

[To John Martin]
November 15, 1977

[* * *] listen, on the poem about Richmond "a very serious fellow" – please never print it in book form. I've written to Winans who accepted it and have asked him to tear it. Steve can't handle it. he's hooked into something besides poetry which makes him weak against almost everything of this sort. I can't say any more about it. just tear the poem or don't publish it. [* * *]

[To Carl Weissner]
November 16, 1977

slow in answering, my ass deep into horses and white wine . . . [* * *]

I do wish to hell, though, that there were some way we could get *Women* going over there. it's the ultimate novel blast of blasts, it should cause riots in the streets. mostly because they will be confused by my viewpoint, which I am also confused about. and now and then I do much leg-pulling and they'll never know when I am pulling the leg or jacking-off the truth or writing it as it is, or was. John says we gotta wait until June. I do wish he could get a copy to you, to see if you might care to translate it. right now it's not in final draft. I would like to see it again and maybe take out a few wrinkles. [* * *]

[To A. D. Winans]
December 3, 1977

[* * *] I'm still writing poems and fighting with Linda Lee. Since she's 34 I'm giving away 23 years but I'm right on in there. Interview of me, with me, in present German *Playboy* but since I can't speak the language I don't know what I said; besides, I was drunk and so was the guy who flew over here. The whole interview was a two day drunk and they layed $650 on me for it. Jesus, me and Rod McKuen. . . . Some day I'll be writing you, "A. D., me and Rod Mc and James Dickey are going fishing in the Cataskills . . ." then *you* can attack me and I'll understand.

Bukowski very rarely went to movies. Here he reports on one directed by François Truffaut.

[To John Martin]
December 12, 1977

here's more poems.

by the way, I went to see the Movie *The Man Who Loved Women* thinking it might be something like our novel *Women*. excuse me, but there's nothing to worry about: ours is more humorous, more insane and more tragic and — the devil knows — more realistic.

got the checks, ah. yes, I should have kept book this year but I had no idea . . . will begin on the first of Jan. I phoned Calif. Fed. Savings because I had torn up my earlier pass books and have no records but the lady informed me that they had no records either and . . . I said, "Suppose I were the income tax people and I asked to examine some of your books?" and she answered, "Well, if they subpoenaed us we'd let them see them." which leaves me nowhere.

I know what your salary to me was, that's fine. and City Lights always sends me a statement of earnings. But the Germans? Christ, I have no idea. I could write them and ask for statements but such things are slow and maybe even impossible. to top that they'd send me total earnings *before* your cut and Carl's cut. now, here's the biggy!: do you have any idea of what I got from them? I'd appreciate a breakdown (looks like I'm having one). I'd never implicate you in any tax investigation but a set of figures from you would really help this damned muddle. also, didn't I receive something from Playboy-New Visions? and not to be *greedy*, ugg, but wasn't there a second payment due Oct. 15 or Jan. 15 or something? I guess I've spoiled your day but I lay a lot of this shit on you because I need help with this and I feel that our relationship while straight on an editor-publisher writer relationship is straight, I ask you to perhaps help me with this on more of a friendship basis. next year I'll be totally competent and professional about the whole thing for my interests and everybody else's.

now *that* was one hell of a poem, wasn't it?, and not the kind I'm fond of writing.

[To Carl Weissner]
December 15, 1977

[* * *] good checks from Germany arriving through Martin via you and the publishers. you are our beloved hit-man. and the money is lovely; I drink better wine, eat out now and then; even bought two new pairs of pants and some shirts the other day, 2 new tires for my car. I can go to the track and lose 30 dollars without having a nightmare, and I'm going to phone my dentist tomorrow. sounds pretty fucking civilized but it's a good change and I have written around 200 poems since Sept., most of them pretty fair. [* * *]

Now I gotta worry about income tax. this life gets wilder and wilder, but the main thing I go on is whether this typewriter is working well or not.

• 1978 •

[To John Martin]
January 6, 1978

[★ ★ ★] I can't help now and then feeling good about *Women*, though, it's going to be an a-bomb in the novel wars when there has been so much nullity and so much peace. forgive me for saying so, but this one is going to ring down some walls and the bitter counter-attackers will at last have something to do.

[To Carl Weissner]
January 22, 1978

[★ ★ ★] oh, you tell your wife that almost all the teeth I have left are in the front. I used to live on one candy bar a day while writing my short stories; candy bar and cheap wine, then the old ten year drunk, and the years of starvation. I used to reach into my mouth with my fingers and pull my teeth out. I would just wiggle a loose tooth for a while and it would work out. or I had teeth that I just picked away at, breaking off chunks. it was interesting and not at all fearful. it really wasn't until 1970 that I started eating better and drinking better. I even went to a dentist a few years back and he looked at the x-rays and said, "I don't understand this. It looked like your teeth gave up and suddenly they decided not to give up."

I haven't heard a thing from the French publisher who suggested the Paris trip. Maybe my letter scared him off. I asked not to be placed into a slick hotel but into a place where the common people lived, the French ordinary, without the American tourist. I also asked not to be fucked with too much. I don't know. Maybe I scared him off. Maybe I can still make Germany. I can afford it but jesus you'd think some of those publishers would kick in a bit; I might do a few tricks for them to help sales – a few, not too many. and maybe a reading to help expenses. but I can make it without aid. we'll see. I hope your back is better by then so we can lift a few together. Linda Lee says hello. she's high on you. when I get drunk I brag on you. but don't worry, I still have the old German reserve; I won't slobber all over you when — if — I arrive.

and Carl, I know that Paris, go or not, is pretty much shit and pretty much hard but so is almost everyplace else, and that type of thing I am used to. the Left Bank means as much to me as east Greenwich Village, and Munich or wherever the hell else would be the same — people and streets and the moil. still it might be nice to have a look — a small yellow notebook to write down streets and places — New York city or New Orleans, Mannheim or Andernach, it's shit in the sewer, cunts, cocks, police, betrayal, madness, joy and something to drink.

the horses are going very well for me. I have devised a system that entails 5 numbers — I will rate each horse in 5 categories and he will have numbers say like this: 2, 7, 4, 3, 6. each contains a meaning, a compilation: on the final odds of the horse, the first number must be *lower* than the odds, the center 3 less than the odds, and the last number near or below the odds, all depending upon the first flash of the toteboard and the last. it's quite quite interesting. and it gets me out of this god damned place and away from the typewriter so I don't have to play professional writer. [★ ★ ★]

[To Carl Weissner]
February 22, 1978

[★ ★ ★] Renate Derschau brought by a couple of copies of *Stern*. Poor Linda Lee Beighle . . . billed as Linda King. she reacted and sent a *cable* to *Stern* . . . I can't blame her. forgive me, but she's a much better soul than Linda King, and such things cut. the photos were good, though. o.k.

I'm still writing nothing but poems. I don't understand it. they are all around me here, dozens of them. I have to go with the tide. the poems are all around me here. at night I type them while drinking wine and now I've got to type them up without the wine stains and errors and get them out of here. I shouldn't complain; it's better than having everything shut off. it fits my battle plan of typing the last poem in the deathbed or wherever it might happen . . .

Linda Lee and I will be leaving L.A. May 9th [i.e. 8th] at 8:15 p.m. and will arrive at Frankfurt May 9th at 3:20 p.m. [* * *] we'll stay 3 weeks [* * *] I think one reading is enough. Linda Lee says she looks forward to meeting you. there are some changes. we are off the beer, just drink wine, German, mostly white and only eat fish and poultry, no red meat. I have come down from 223 pounds to 196 but drink more than ever. we should try to slow down just a bit in Germany, though. got to face the judge tomorrow morning at 8:30 a.m. jesus, what an hour to face a drunk driving rap. but I've stood before that man many times. I hope he's a nice old fellow. oh yeah.

we may make Paris in September *if* the Frenchies come through with one round trip ticket. I don't mind spending dollars to see the Fatherland but the Frogs are going to have to dance a little before I do the Paris journey.

well, listen, friend, I have to get typing some of these fucking poems up. and I must thank you again and forever, Carl, for translating my stuff so that they like it so much and for pushing Charlie Bukowski and for collecting bills and knocking down doors. you are the miracle man.

[To John Martin]
March 9, 1978

[* * *] The trip to Germany will be low-profile, easy and I intend to avoid the hale guzzlers. I drink for my pleasure, not my image, or their image of me. My health is better now than it has been for 40 years. I have no intention of tossing it away.

Women is going to land like an H-bomb into all this literary serenity. [* * *]

[To Carl Weissner]

March 12, 1978 within the dwindling years after the death of the sun leeving only the father under der Holy Ghost . . .

Hello Carl –

Perhaps a little too much white wine tonight. Linda Lee in bed re-reading *A Pavilion of Women*[1] and me out here (3:11 a.m.) smoking and sipping and lucking upon some Mozart upon the radio. And I get worried about coming to Germany but then I think, fuck it, I'll let it slide. And I remember when you came over here I was terrified to meet you at the airport because I'd never been to one and I didn't know how and I was afraid I couldn't do it. Now I've been in and out of dozens of airports (quite suddenly) and anyhow – thanks for sending magazines such as *Stern* and etc. as they come out Bukowskivana. What I'm writing about, however, is I intend to enclose $2 and if *Stern* ever comes out with an apology-retraction for the Linda King Linda Lee fuck-up (as demanded by cable), please mail said copy, much thanks. We have a German bookstore here but they dragass about 2 months behind time. For instance, as of this date, they are only stocked up on and up to *Stern* #3. So, if they ever come out with their thing, please mail, o.k.? Letter from Unc. Heinrich, has been in hospital for months, heart trouble, now out, he will be *90* years old this March 15. I hope he lasts until I can say hello to him. I hope I last until . . .

Linda Lee says that we will "defile" you. I tell her that you are already that way. She says, maybe so in a German way but that we shall defile you in the American way. I hope so. Actually, both she and myself prefer a quiet and easy and gentle visit. Hello to your son and your wife. Tell your son I come to shake his hand in warmth as one German boy grown old to another German boy to carry on.

---

1. *Pavilion of Women* by Pearl S. Buck (New York, 1946).

[To Hank Malone]
March 13, 1978

All right, you're my literary shrink. like, you know, living in east Hollywood is pretty damned splendid because all that messes with one are the hookers, cops, crazies – black, white and yellow, and there are poets around but only those who haven't made it and when they make it they move up to Frisco. as per the door-knockers I have lessened them and the phone has become unlisted. the problem with the door-knockers is that they are all quite similar, they say almost the same words as the phone-ringers, and it gets strange and fearful as if they had all been sent by the same Central Parrot Society. I was never one for mixing socially and maybe now that I've had some luck with the writing, that hasn't changed, although some may think my disdain for them is related to the luck I've had with the writing lately. but if I acted the way they wanted me to I'd be them and I'd be knocking on doors.

Finished a novel, *Women*, I guess I told you . . . finished it last Sept. Martin says not until June 1978. he can't keep up with me. since then I've been on the poem-kick and have probably written a couple hundred. when *Women* comes out I might get shot like Larry Flynt (of *Hustler*). I'm off the beer, have switched to good white wine, drink *plenty* of that and only eat fish and poultry; my other habits are about the same, only I'm down to *one* woman now, much less travail, but, of course, I still get pretty low-down now and then; I guess the mechanism is set that way. have come down from 223 pounds and I now weigh in at 193 – from a 44 waist to a 37. there are lots of fighting years ahead; working on the left hook and the counter-punch. going to take a hop to Germany in May. intend to return. they caught me drunk driving on the Harbor Freeway last month. I now go to the Drunk Driver's Improvement School. what a turnip patch that is. the instructor talks about the problems he has with his wife. last week he drew a diagram of the female sexual mechanism upon the blackboard and gave lessons on how to eat pussy, although most of his students already seemed well-versed in the art of.

. . . all these poems running out of my ass now . . . I get somewhat worried about the short story . . . have only done one since last Sept. but I go with the tide, maybe it's a rip tide but you don't fight those either.

yes, I know about Celine. they stole his bike, his hog, busted up his berry patch because of supposed anti-semitism and Nazism. Hamsun got the same hard boot. see Ezra. it's surprising how many of the good writers got caught and hacked like this. what people don't realize [is] that it is hard for a good writer to go with what is an overwhelming political Thou Shalt Believe. they have to go the other way simply out of their natures feeling that most of the people around them are wrong most of the time. I'm not saying that the right is always right or that the left is all that's left. I'm just saying that these men puked up against the obvious. ah, well . . . [★ ★ ★]

[To Carl Weissner]
April 3, 1978

[★ ★ ★] The Academy awards are on t.v. tonight, Linda Lee watches and I sit with ear plugs in. movies don't do it for me; I even find the so-called pretty good ones pretty bad. they miss somewhere, they seldom get down near the bone. it's a giant shuck, the whole entertainment field, and the masses suffer brain damage from eating the shit. earplugs are a blessing. sometimes when the rock stars come on I bless the gods for these motherfucking red rubber plugs. I still prefer to select the areas I move around in and if people think me an egotist and a crank, they may be right – but I have some thoughts for them too. amen.

Mannheim dull or not is o.k. I don't expect a circus over there. I expect people to be walking around, most of them with arms and legs, most of them dressed in clothing, some of them constipated, some of them frenzied, most of them sleepwalking and a few of them all right. we, I, don't want to stay at your place for 2 days, that to me is an imposition. maybe we could find a place around the corner and take you and yours out to a few meals. you've got your work to do. I would enjoy drinking some wine with you and talking easy, lazy. I think we should room somewhere nearby, a city nearby Mannheim and we can bus about and take our little tourist photos, got another AE-1 and am trying not to lose it. also, like a god damned writer and unlike I do around here I'll probably carry a little green notebook and write down names of streets, places, so forth. I'm not much of a sight-seer, I'm mostly a lazy man except that I type about as much as I sleep. got to see unc, though, he's 90, has a bad heart and I want to go *very* gentle with him, no drinking around him, no hippies, no door-knockers. [★ ★ ★]

[To Hank Malone]
April 25, 1978

[★ ★ ★] Read at the university of Wisconsin, Milwauk., on Ape 17 but they got me too drunk before the reading and I drank during. I think I blew the whole god damned trick but I got the check, a grand plus air, so that will teach them.

I get plenty of mail, most of it thin and sick – my readers Some of them act as if they own me. Many of them claim I have saved their lives, which doesn't perk me up one tit's worth: Billy Graham and Bob Hope have probably saved some lives too.

Going to Germany in May. Taking my girlfriend if we don't split before then. You know how human relationships don't work.

[★ ★ ★] Physically and spiritually I am feeling pretty high lately; I used to be afraid of that; now when it comes I embrace it like a beautiful virgin; I know that the other – that whore – is going to come back quickly enough. [★ ★ ★]

[To John Martin]
May 3, 1978

this is probably the last writing I'll send you until I get back from Germany. life gets more curious; I peek under the edge of the tent: clowns in there, clowns outside, but not very funny. but gimme a little credit, Mencken, I ain't formed no schools or preached any directions nor have I taken guru-shape. there's hope and when a man has hope he's got hold of ¾'s of the ball of string. o, yes. [★ ★ ★]

[To Carl Weissner]
May 3, 1978

yes, it's here on the ticket: 3:20 p.m. I don't worry about the terrorists, if they think I am important enough to be killed, well, that's it. actually, I'll pass through without a whisper. no, not exactly, a German stewardess who knows us might be on the same flight and a photographer,

I forget his name, will probably be clicking away. don't be alarmed, don't pose. [★ ★ ★]

All right, not much time. cleaning things up. Carl, even if anything and everything turns to shit it's still o.k. no mountain climbing. I'd like to meet your wife and your boy. sit quietly. I should be tired but I'm not. But still, vast spaces of air and easiness are wonderful. [★ ★ ★]

[To Carl Weissner]
June 6, 1978

Well, Linda took another week or so off and we layed around and drank some more and played the horses but 5 or 6 weeks at 24 hours a day together can be murderous and Linda's physic pyschic [sic] somebody says that thereby makes her a saint and I suppose she is. anyhow, this is one of my first nights alone at the old machinegun and it's good that it's still cranking . . . 4 or 5 new poems, not too bad, I think . . . one about a Rhine cruise, so I know I've been to Germany. Got a letter off to Unc down on Privat Strasse 1, refused to open the door to some visitors who claim they are my friends . . . had a sign out: "WORKING . . . please call at another time, thanx, Hank . . ." they saw the sign, heard the typer, knocked anyhow. never catch a writer working, jesus christ, it's shameful, and if you do catch him working, it doesn't matter, he can do it at another time, he can do it anytime. Right, Carl? a plumber or something, you don't fuck with him. you don't stop a fireman or a dentist, but a writer??? shit, it's all a shuck, my god, every man's a poet . . .

By the way, Martin gets 20%, I told you 10. He used to get 10. Linda dislikes him, thinks he is fucking me, so I told you 10 so she wouldn't start the shit. I appreciate her concern but I don't want to end up like Celine . . . bitching and bitching against editors and publishers. the idea is to write about something else. by the way, thanks again for the *complete* rundown of finances . . . must have taken you two weeks but it keeps the air clear for me. [★ ★ ★] the radio's on. I'm alone. I've got to get alone, finally. I fill on the walls. people confuse me, crowds of people. they are all so sane. they all know what to do. what to say. the assholes terrify me. yet, I am able to write about them, about it. that's luck or I'd have to hide in a madhouse. in fact, that's what I'm rather doing. I'm stronger than the people and I'm weaker. I see what they see, only I can't use it; what's honey to them is sawdust to me. well, fuck a pig in the ass! listen to me weep! [★ ★ ★]

[To Hank Malone]
June 27, 1978

Your stuff is getting better, you are banking your shots in with more ease and laughter – that way is better because if you are telling the truth it's done without preaching and if you're telling a lie you didn't mean it because you weren't trying. so. [★ ★ ★]

Things rough on the human relationship scale right now right here. she is a good person but I am not. well, not really. it's just that I don't understand things. like proclamations, reality, subject matter, excreatia [sic], trips to Paris and yellow submarines. it's just that so many things interest so many people and they don't interest me. it causes a grinding, a gnawing, a wearing away of the parts. eliminating people is more important than finding them. the walls are my honeys, the walls are my whores.

how's that for a speech from the pulpit?

Hang onto Michigan, Malone, while I watch them unwind down that long stretch, the strain of numbers while the geese paddle senselessly . . .

ah, boy, the taste of the arrow ain't no mushroom.

[To John Martin]
July 1, 1978

Still more poems . . ., that particular mind-state holds and there's nothing I can do about it.

The lack of good fat prose worries me but there have been, and still are, worse things to worry about, if we must do that.

Working on drawings [★ ★ ★]

Women is my proudest and best work. The arrival, that day, of that book in the mail will be the day the sun bows down to me. Not too much, I hope.

p.s. – We have a long journey together, Ace. Do you think you can hold up? Better cut down on the boozeroni . . . yeh . . .[1]

[To John Martin]
July 16, 1978

Yes, John: I've heard it against Black Sparrow from my "friends" for some time. And I figure you've rejected them. It's the nature of the writer to believe it's the editor's fault if they aren't published. They never consider that their stuff might simply stink. I don't listen to them much and get rid of them as soon as it's possibly able to be done in a fairly decent manner . . . To hell with them . . . (bad grammer above . . . ah, well . . .)

But for *our* sakes we ought to have a working method. I sign a contract with you for each book; all I want is what is in that contract, nothing extra. So the semi-yearly or yearly statement takes care of that. Nobody likes to work in the dark. And your idea of continuing to pay me in spite of what occurs, we don't need. Just what is due. If the sales fall off, let the checks fall off. And if you die or sell Black Sparrow, then whoever takes over and continues to sell my books should pay me my just accord as per contract. I don't ask any more than any other writer, nor do I ask less. If this is understood then we have no worries. My job is writing, yours is editing and publishing. Let's keep the air clear and neither of us will go down the tube, together or separately.

I await *Women* unlike I've ever awaited any other book. As I wrote it I could feel it happening – that certain carving into the page with certain words in a way that you feel the power and the magic and the luck. I don't think you've ever taken a gamble like this, nor have I. We've rolled for the works here, knowing damn well about the rancor and bitterness and good old simple white hatred this thing would cause, and in a way while writing it I even now and then gave them a little flick here and there so that they could scream and bitch just some more. We'll hang together – you from the right branch, me from the left. O.K? Let's get the son of a bitch out. I meet people in the marketplace and liquor stores, they keep asking me, "When's *Women* coming out?" This is our big baby, John . . . I

---

1. John Martin does not drink alcohol.

congratulate you on your courage . . . some of those literary tea cup ladies and boys just ain't gonna like you very much now. Me? I'm used to it. And please don't think I'm against you. You were there when nobody else was. I don't forget.

Linda isn't against you either. She hears the bad mouths. We know where that comes from . . . She sends regards. [* * *]

[To Carl Weissner]
July 16, 1978

[* * *] On page 25 of the German photo trip . . . of course, it isn't going to be what anybody expected, for my mouth is in my ears and my eyes are in my asshole and my asshole is in my mouth. o, boy. anyhow. then I am interrupted by the poem and the racetrack and the bottle. only to say, no excuses – everything as it always was.

Linda has not really gotten to eating again since Germany. I watched her. I knew she was starting too fast like a child broken into a candy storehouse, she'd have to pay. I've got this crazy food thing. I've starved so many years, got raised in the depression. I just can't stand to see the stuff thrown against the ceiling. I was very glad that you were about to clean up people's mental excesses toward food when their bellies couldn't follow up. And with food that *expensive* . . . you were a brave man and you did the brave thing. I don't give a damn *who's* paying for a thing, I don't like to see it beat to Death with a stick.

Jack Micheline by a couple of nights ago. He talked and drank and read me his poems and showed me his drawings, then slept on the couch and puked all over the place, missing the huge wastebasket I had placed right where his head was supposed to be. [* * *]

It's been a long journey and a clean, hard, decent fight. I'll always remember you, baby, in your white tennis shoes and your good quietness and your good laugh, and your honor and your knowledgeability. You've got it. You'll keep it. You drive a good car and a good life.

[To William Packard]
July 16, 1978

Back from Germany. West to a racetrack there and a couple of castles. Racetrack had no toteboard. My whole method of play revolves around the toteboard. The castles were cheaper. The last issue of the *NYQ* was the best – #21. People are getting to write more and more like I do.

Packed them in at the hall at Hamburg, 1200 with 300 turned away. Drank 2 bottles of wine and sang it to them. My German editor told me no writer of books had drawn such a crowd since the fellow who had written the book "Mein Kamph" (spell?). Newspaper and television interviews. Saw myself as tv newscast ... American writer arrives ... I wave off questions, snarl answers, look mean and hungover, hair in eyes, looked *authentic* somehow.

Anyhow, I'm back here where it's quiet and Mailer and Capote and Vidol (spell?). Working on a book about the trip. Some guy took 3,000 photos. I'm not sure I can do it but have begun to beat the ribbon, first 25 pages done. May go to Paris in September for the French boys. May not. May turn into a complete shit. May not.

That's it. 96 degrees here. Sitting in my shorts. Have fixed these poems for your eyes for better or worse. 96 degrees here. Smoking Sher Bidi's from Jabalpur, India and caressing the good German white wine, Bernkastel Reisling (spell? O, I can't), Brooks too Broad for Leaping, you know ...[1]

[To A. D. Winans]
July 27, 1978

[* * *] bad night last night, right, no left arm tightened up, hurt like mad, from thumb to elbow. no sleep, no great thoughts. they just send you pain now and then and it sits on you. most people say mental pain is the worst but at least you can fight your way out of that; the other way you depend on outside sources and they may be wrong. I thought in terms of stroke but today the doc said it was nerve-ending fuck-up

---

1. Cf. A. E. Housman's poem, "With Rue My Heart Is Laden."

generated by the spine. now that's not so bad. except I drank 3 bottles of wine and it didn't ease a thing. enough.

the German trip, yes. I only wanted to do one reading to help the cause: mine. read in Hamburg. there don't seem to be so many haters over there. they seem to be trying to ingest the poem and get what there is. they listen quite carefully and seem to laugh when it seems the place to do so. the German girls are quiet in a beautiful way. and the men have a quiet reserve. it was, it created a feeling of no-con and a sensible generosity. [* * *]

The photographer who recorded Bukowski and Linda Lee Beighle's trip to Germany was Michael Montfort. These photos were subsequently published with text by Bukowski as Shakespeare Never Did This *(1979, 1995).*

[To Carl Weissner]
August 1, 1978

[* * *] Still on page 30 on the travel book; the photos rather staid — don't tell Michael I said this — they need a drink or a goose in the ass. anyhow, I might save the thing? so putting off getting into it I wrote 12 poems this week, most of them 3 or 4 pages long and about half of them pretty fair. If I ever go to France there'll be no photographer along and nobody is going to plan me a little picture tour. I know people mean well, they want me on a boat or looking at a castle. I think slowly. next time it's my turn. I felt as if I were tied with ropes and drugged most of the German trip. in France if I wanna sit at a fucking table and drink for 3 days I'll do so. unless a man's nature is allowed to reach the surface it's no good being anywhere. well, enough of that bitching. [* * *]

Barbet Schroeder was later to direct Barfly. *The documentary here referred to is* General Idi Amin Dada: Self Portrait *(1974).*

[To Carl Weissner]
August 24, 1978

[★ ★ ★] Barbet Schroeder, the French film maker, by the other night. We drank, of course. I don't know if you're familiar. He's done *More, Koko* and a documentary on the African dictator, the crazy and original one. Sends so many bodies down the river the crocodiles can't eat them all and it fucks up the power supply and the lights go out. He wants to do one of my long short stories, a 90 minute work. I don't know if I have anything that might fit that length. [★ ★ ★]

Saggitaire phoned. Want me to come to Paris. I said, "o.k., write details." So it's probably Paris around Sept. 16 or 17 for 5 or 6 days. They will get air fare and hotel, including Linda. They speak of meeting the press on the 18th and going on the # one t.v. station on the 22. Should do. [★ ★ ★]

My tax accountant over the other night. He said that I was antagonistic. He wants to talk about his soul and tell me how intelligent he is. I don't want to make a life time friendship, I just want him to tell me how to save money. That's what I'm paying him for. I think I'm getting guidance from a bum. It fits my theory that most people can't do anything near what they claim they can do. [★ ★ ★]

Bukowski's daughter was 14 years old in 1978.

[To Marina Bukowski]
September 6, 1978

Hello Marina:

Happy birthday.

Enclosed an m.o. Get yourself something. You know best. There has been a great deal to do around here, writing and otherwise. Leaving for Europe on the 16th, will be back in 3 weeks plus. Meanwhile, I've got to learn to speak French, haha, and German, haha. Will probably not get to see you until I get back.

I hope going back to school is not too tedious for you. I never liked it.

o.k.

[To Carl Weissner]
November 3, 1978

Has Mikey burned down east Germany yet? And you tell Voltrout, Linda's love and mine to her for her hospitality and her understanding, her gentleness. And like I said over the phone, thanks to you for getting part of the hotel bill; now we know why it was so small, and thanks even though you shouldn't have, you bastard. And thanks for driving us for hours and days and suffering with us and drinking with us and living through air-line fuck-ups with us. Now your suffering due to us is over for a while. [★ ★ ★]

I was dissatisfied with the first 50 pages I wrote on the first German trip and I'm now writing it all over again, up to page 40. It's looser this time with more madness. I was guided too much by the photographs the first time. I've got to write my thing and just hope the photos fit . . . *Women* still at the printer's in Ann Arbor, Michigan. This is the slowest book getting off the blocks. The lag is maddening. *I finished the novel in August 1977.* [★ ★ ★]

Hope Ginsberg isn't screwing up your brain cells too much. With that guy it's one line at a time, then forget that line and go to the next, which will have nothing to do with the line which preceded it or the one to follow . . .

Bukowski and Linda Lee Beighle moved to their new house in San Pedro in November 1978.

[To Carl Weissner]
November 11, 1978

[★ ★ ★] I am still fighting the little horrors and fuck-ups of moving but am levelling out now and trying to work my way toward the typer, the only normal place for this abnormal fleshpot.

Women still not out . . .

This is one fine town; it lacks some violence and madness but I have enough of that to compensate, and the harbor is fine and the god damned boats, the fresh fish each day, the wine at night, and still can get to the racetracks. Linda downstairs reading a book on organic gardening. the dream is to grow vegetables out front in an attempt to beat the mortgage rap. many new things and it's about time . . .

Butch the cat has cost me over one hundred bucks trying to get his head patched after a cat fight. he tore off the 3rd bandage tonight. got to take him back to the clip-joint vet place tomorrow . . . [★ ★ ★]

[To John Martin]
November 18, 1978

The new check looked damn good; I think with that and with my hustle on the side we might pull it off, for a while anyhow, and meanwhile it's an outrageous experience. Now that I look back I don't think I should have taken such a big bite of pie but the 2 trips to Europe this year left me a bit more confused than usual. If it bites into the tax load to a decent extent then it'll be worth it; better into real estate than into govt. And I can always pull out and get something back. And we lucked it getting it at 10 percent just a month or so ago and now mortgage rates are 11 percent and rising. Maybe it's all good luck. It's sure a long way from that $1.25 shack in Atlanta, reaching and waving at that broken electric cord, playing with suicide, freezing, starving, no out. The gods are giving me plenty of variety and I guess they aren't through with me yet. The test is always there and it will always be there, yes, yes.

o.k., back to the travelogue. [★ ★ ★]

[To Carl Weissner]
November 28, 1978

[★ ★ ★] Went in today and hit them with 2 mortgage payments instead of one. I hope to get a year ahead on payments so when lean times come I will have time to make certain moves. Meanwhile, the downstairs bedroom is a good place for drunken guests. Myself, I fell down the other night against the edge of the fireplace, really crushed my side in, much blood and it took me a good hour or so to get up the stairway to my bed. I am still in shit poor shape, hard to sleep with the pain and so forth . . . the travelogue thing proceeds, should soon be finished.

Got proofs from *Hustler* on my story "Break-In." I discovered an error, I had a 32 magnum in there and there isn't any such thing so I phoned the copy editor and told him to change it to 38 magnum and while talking to him I learned something: Larry Flynt ain't just kidding about his religious stance. The copy editor told me that my story had several "god damns" in it and that Larry wouldn't allow God to be used like that in his mag so my people instead of saying "god damn" would have to end up saying "damn." Also 20 other lines deleted. [★ ★ ★]

Oh, thanks for the rundown on the Big Book, I like to know what's happening so my mind is clear for the old piano. payments are all in order; I realize John shouldn't get payment for *Notes* but since he only takes a 20 percent cut out of U.S. sales I told him it would be all right. People like Ferlinghetti, for instance, take 50 percent plus the agent's fees.

We would really like to see your family over here while we have this house and the big yard in front, big hedge to hide us from the street and neighbors who just say hello, and Mike would LOVE the FIREPLACE!!! and Voltrout and Linda could go bathing at Cabrillo beach while you and I worried about survival of the written word and ourselves. But I know you'd need some angle to get over here, a grant, something, and maybe you could only come alone which would be fine but not as good as with the good Voltrout and the jumping fireman Mikey. [★ ★ ★]

[To Carl Weissner]
December 6, 1978

[* * *] The typing is worse than usual, real cold tonight, will hit 29 degrees, which is cold for Calif. Linda screamed over the phone that the walnut tree was going to die and I should cover it with a sheet and tie it and I went up this rickety-ass ladder with sheet on pitchfork, I swung in the wind, the bastard was too tall for me, let it die, me swaying in this sky, thinking, all I need now is a broken hip or leg; I've just mended from falling into the fireplace. was never crazy for walnuts anyhow. So that's why my fingers are cold, just got in from out there . . .

Had some luck the other night, going through old contracts, came across this one I signed with Ferlinghetti on *Erections* in Jan. 1971. And I saw where I had made him cross out the 50–50 deal on foreign rights and write in: "25% publisher, 75% author" . . . And, of course, I had forgotten all about that, so I jumped to the machine and wrote Nancy Peters about it and she says, o.k., sorry, we'll straighten it, we owe you $4,500 from last year, we're broke, but don't worry we'll get it to you . . . So, there's a break, I must been thinking in 1971. On the *Notes* contract it reads 50/50 though. But on *Erections* it's going to be a big help through the French, Italian, German, Swedish sales of that book. so, some luck is coming and I'll take it all . . . [* * *]

[To William Packard]
December 31, 1978 10 p.m.

I am sitting in this place in San Pedro, strapped with mortgage payments because my tax accountant says it's a good thing. "Look, man," I told him, "you don't understand writers. This thing is going to kill me." I've got this old desk here and I can step out on this balcony and see the harbor lights. Much trouble here – fell into the fireplace drunk the other night, really got scalded and tore a few muscle sheaths. My girlfriend put cat medicine on my side . . . 2 trips to Europe this year. last one I am sitting in Paris and my French editor says, "you want to go see Sartre?" No, I tell him. I got up and got shit-ass drunk on national French tv before 50 million Frenchmen. I am having Henry Miller luck in Europe; well, not Henry Miller luck, say one-quarter Henry Miller luck . . . novel, *Women*, finally out. trying to do a screenplay to be directed by Barbet Schroeder, writing short stories for *Hustler*, trying to change my luck at the racetrack. I like San Pedro, the blacks, Mexicans, whites, all mix without much trouble or tension – so far. I mean, since I've been here. Europe is clean and quick and a dollar there buys about what a quarter does here. The whores of Paris lovely, lovely . . . I've got to do another 15 years of good, hard writing – let's see: 58 and 15 equals . . . well, best not to think about that . . . Met a guy at the track the other day. "Man," he said, "we sure miss you down at the post office! you were really funny, man!" the "funny" he was talking about were those sounds I was making from the cross . . . Got your card. Packard, I don't know where the fuck your love is . . . O.k. . . .

p.s. – I guess you've moved by now and this will be intercepted by a batch of Porto Rican pimps. O.k., they'll like it. I do too.

• 1979 •

[To Louise Webb]
January 2, 1979

Hello Lou:

I lost your card letter, finally found it.

No, I hadn't heard you had a heart attack; you keep taking those pills. Marina Louise is now 14 years old; she's a tall gentle girl.

I'm living with a good woman, Linda Lee, and have moved out of east Hollywood, at last . . . Got into this home in San Pedro because my tax accountant talked me into it. But I may have bitten off more than I can handle – mortgage payments simply hellishly high. Big old house, large front yard, there's a balcony outside this room that overlooks the harbor, a working harbor with ships coming and going; fresh fish every day, 2 cats, a lemon tree, a tangerine tree, fig tree, other trees. I find that I am still able to type here, just finished a travelogue of my last trip to Europe. Went to Europe twice this year, got drunk and vile on national French television. Much luck with my work in Germany, France. Also work translated into Italian, Swedish, Spanish and Denmark dickering for some work or other. But it's a recent windfall and may not last. I'll really miss this old big house if I have to resell. And it's about time I had luck with a good woman. Linda Lee is a good match for me. If Jon were alive he'd really get his kicks out of seeing me live in this place after all those small rooms and courts. After all, it was you and Jon who really got me started. Remember those days? The presses? Breaking in shipment . . . the flood . . . fire . . . attack . . . moving from city to city. I often talk about you two. those crazy editor-publishers, starving to bring out these beautiful and immortal printing jobs . . . books that people now look at in wonderment . . . remember our nights of drinking? with the roaches climbing the walls? pages of Bukowski stacked in the bathtub and sky-high around the walls? It was a crazy and magic time, and the good old *Outsider* too . . . never quite a magazine like that . . . I no longer hear from William Corrington, he wrote a novel about the Civil war and went to Hollywood, and that was it. I hear he is now studying politics and wants to be Governor of Louisiana. I've written 3 novels now, one just out called *Women*. Also a few books of short stories and quite a few books of poems. I want to go out writing, though, and now with this mortgage on my back I will damned well have to. There's no stopping for me anyhow, it's ingrained . . .

I know that New Orleans is bad for your emphysema but I think it's the place for you spiritually. When I think of you and Jon, I think New Orleans. I'm glad you're working at an art shop on Bourbon street. You are a New Orleans institution, a grand lady. There should be a place there for you always, Gypsy Lou Webb. Remember standing in the cold trying to hawk those paintings on the sidewalk? They ought to write songs about you. Please try to feel as good as possible. I guess you know old Henry Miller is still alive? His son wrote me a while (Larry) and told me that I was the world's greatest writer. I told him to look over his shoulder and he'd find him. (He lives with Henry.)

So we're still fighting from this seaport town, still trying to get the world down. I still drink too much. Recently fell down against the side of the fireplace, drunk, then smashed the coffee table. Linda Lee put cat medicine on my side. This cat Butch got messed up in a cat fight, cost us $200 to put him back together. Then the front wheels fell off of my 67 Volks. but as *you* know, there's always trouble. We go on for a while . . . Sorry I waited so long in answering . . . have been searching for your letter for days. It was damned good to hear from you. may the gods and the luck be with you . . .

[To Carl Weissner]
January 2, 1979

got your telegram, much thanks, and a lucky and good new year to you and Mikey and Valtrout . . . Are you going to translate the novel (*Women*)? if so, maybe I better xerox the sections Martin cut out, maybe you'd like to use them, I don't know. I feel maybe the novel got a little long for John M. so some of the *Women* bit the dust. let me know. of course we hope Lutz takes the travelogue. I have submitted it to City Lights here, maybe Lutz should know this? I talked Martin into it, although he wanted to do it. [* * *]

Barbet is here and we are trying to get into the screenplay but it seems like all we do is get into the wine. [★ ★ ★]

shit, this sure sounds like a business letter but sometimes they have to be written. o.k., now going down to listen to *The Honeymooners* on TV...

[To Carl Weissner]
February 20, 1979

[★ ★ ★] Trimmed ⅕ of fig tree today, looking up into sky, branches falling on head... began to see white and green lights... took a breather... went into house and smoked ten beedies... About half-finished with screenplay with Barbet Schroeder to direct and film. He likes it better as I go on. He says, "The beginning is quite depressive..." So now a few laughs have come along... somehow... but it's called *Barfly*, about that period in my life when I just sat on a bar stool for years. Parts of that just can't be too god damned happy...

On the Frankfurt thing, sure yes, of course... Linda loves to travel... We're hoping for the Park Hotel again, but if we have to hang out in Frankfurt, o.k. [★ ★ ★]

[To Gerald Locklin]
March 15, 1979

[★ ★ ★] On *Women*, a little tragedy there. Prefer you keep it fairly quiet. Like you know, I tell John Martin to go ahead and correct my grammar but this time he went too far. I should have read the proofs more carefully but am lazy. But when the book came out I read it. Shit, man. I guess he thinks I can't write. he threw shit in. Like I like to say, "he said," "she said." that's enough for me. But he threw stuff in, like "he retorted," "he said cheerfully," "I shrugged," "she seemed to be sore." Shit, it goes on and on... There's even one place where a woman had on a green dress and he put her into a blue dress. At least he didn't change her sexual organs. Think of playing with Faulkner like that? Anyhow, I climbed him

127

pretty hard for it and so the 2nd edition will read on a back page somewhere: "second edition, revised." [★ ★ ★]

[To Carl Weissner]
March 24, 1979

I haven't heard from the Italians so I suppose the trip is off. I think they must have had the idea I was queer enough to leak promotional blood for free.

Thanks for word on *Fuck Machine*. I'll kind of slip it off on City Lights so it will scare them into knowing I have my ear to the ground. Montfort is having some trouble with Ferlinghetti. He went up there with his photographs and Ferling. refused to see him that day because he had gotten drunk with Yevtushenko the night before. Further scam is Yev. was upset and screamed because there was no mirror in his dressing room. Also he demanded mention in a newspaper column that he was chasing women. Me, I think a man is wiser running from women than chasing them. Anyhow, I don't know if the scam is true or not on Yev. but anyhow M.M. is back with his photos and no contract. Maybe we'll go someplace else or maybe we'll forget it. Lutz might be enough for us. Paranoia everywhere. I've had people scream at me that I'm not treating M. Montfort right on the book. I don't know what the hell they're talking about. I'm offering him half, and I know that the book would sell without the photos but that the photos would not sell without the prose, so I don't see how I'm particularly laying anybody open.

I am re-writing the screenplay, taking out the bad first parts. No problems with Barbet, yet. I've agreed with his criticisms except in a couple of places where he didn't quite understand what I was doing.

The January tour sounds all right, ugg, all those *egos*, if that doesn't develop into something sick I'll not only be surprised I'll be rebom. It's all right with me if we don't have to sleep on the bus together, the whole ego gang. I mean, there's got to be a hotel room each night. If that's understood, o.k. But why in January?

Linda and I send luck and love to the Mannheim gang.

Oh, I have 3 *new* tires on my car, first time in my life. And I bought a new German cross (medal) for my windshield, real thing, $30 from the Alpine Village, a German tourist place up the freeway 5 minutes. You ought to see this one shop. An old gal sits there among this memorabilia: helmets, guns, medals, bayonets. Eva Braun's brooch and bracelet are there (documented) and can be had for 5,000 dollars. Linda wants it . . .

[To John Martin]
April 1, 1979

The screenplay is taking longer than I expected but I should soon be back to normal. A few poems enclosed. Did some more last night which are better and will send along soon.

You said you were going to send the new proofs of the 2nd edition of *Women* a couple of weeks back. Nothing has arrived.

Also, somebody told me they were at a university in Tucson and they saw much Bukowski material. Is this the univ. with our archives? I've heard nothing from them. At first it was going to be 10 grand every two years, then it got down to 4 grand for the bunch, and now I hear nothing. Do you think it unkindly of me to ask?

[* * *] I've been drinking too much lately and have made plans to cut it down somewhat. Also there have been some rough seas on the home front here. Everything seems to get in the way of the writing but maybe it creates it too. The seas seem to be smooth now. Back to the movie. Fante is now writing something called *How to Write a Screenplay*. He's one wonderful person.

[To Carl Weissner]
April 23, 1979

[* * *] I did it. I finally finished the screenplay. Took me 3 months. So far I am calling it *The Rats of Thirst*. It's a short section of my life when I sat around on bar stools, starving and crazed. Now I am just crazed. The screenplay is fairly violent but accurate and it might even be humorous, though in writing it I never intended it to be any one of these things. I don't know what I intended it to be. Anyhow, I'm now back on the good old poem again. Sent a few to the French mag *Nomades*. It is easier to write poems while drunk and I like the easy way. Drank 4 bottles of

German white Saturday night after a good day at the race track. Linda is fine. Everything is all right around here, I mean as much as it can get all right. I might slide back into the short story again – the short story has always been a good friend of mine. The next novel, I feel, is still two or three years off – I mean before I start writing it.

I dig in the old garden a bit now and then. The neighbors like it when they see me doing that. A man working in his garden is not a dangerous man (they think). They've heard some wild screaming nights over here when I've gone mad on wine and run about the house naked, up and down the stairs, falling, cursing and all that. They prefer me in the garden. [* * *]

[To John Martin]
April 24, 1979

Here are some poems.

I've heard from two sources that Sagittaire is going to fold. I wonder how this will affect royalties? My guess is that they are certainly selling books and as long as they sell them they ought to pay up. According to Garnier: "Looks like Hachette, the biggies who sponsor the Sagittarious endeavor, got fed up with the publishers' 'bad moves'. Looks like they paid too much money to get your books! At least that's part of the problem. They had to shed some twenty grand, or so they say, to secure your remaining opus. And now Hachette says they can't tolerate this, it's got to stop."

I have no way of knowing how much you are selling book rights for but if you are asking too much it could be bad for me. As you know, I've agreed to let you jump from 10 percent to 20 percent because you do a hell of a lot of work free for me, archives and many things I don't know about. I don't mind this extra 10 percent, it's as if you were my American agent, and friend. Linda wanted me to limit you to 10 percent but I said, no. A few of these writers who you *don't* publish come around and speak bitterly of you but I know damn well they'd say you were great, one of the greatest if you published their work. Meanwhile Linda listens and becomes confused.

I want my head clear so I can write. In a sense it is easier writing in a small room and talking to the mice and drinking cheap beer. What comes to the top comes there undisturbed. Now there is really more pressure but I'm going to beat that bastard too: Mr. Pressure. I get all these letters from people who claim I have saved their lives; little do they realize I am still trying to save my own. Yes, I'm drinking, and rambling. Take it easy.

[To Carl Weissner]
April 27, 1979

[★ ★ ★]On *Shakespeare Never Did This*, Michael Montfort is trying to squeeze Ferlinghetti out of his usual 8 percent but I don't know if anything has been done yet. Is it possible to give Ferlinghetti the English speaking rights instead of just the American? The book will sell twice as much this way. [★ ★ ★]

I think I told you I finished the screenplay. Barbet is out sniffing around for money. All he needs is a half million or a million, haha. I think it's a lively work and if it ever comes to being produced it will be entertaining but maybe offensive to certain types who can't understand laughter through violence. [★ ★ ★]

[To John Martin]
May 7, 1979

Well, I hope everybody's feeling better and that we can get on with the game.

I understand that now there's a paper strike going on. I went out and bought 6 packs of 200 pgs of typer paper. How's that for a 6-pack? So that ought to last me a month or two . . . but how are you going to print books? The little darlings will think that you don't like them . . .

[To John Martin]
May 8, 1979

Here's a copy of *Barfly*, the screenplay. As you know, I did quite a bit of barstool duty between the ages of 25 and 35. This screenplay takes in 4 or 5 nights or days (or maybe more) from that time. Right now Barbet is off to Europe looking for various sources of money to get it into motion and unto film. He claims he can do it for a half million. I have an idea he will get the money and that he will direct the film and get it done. he seems to know how to do such things.

Anyhow, the screenplay is available for book production. There are no restrictions in the contract on this and Barbet says he has no objections, and there is no money to be paid to him, although, of course, credits must be given.

So read it when you get time and if you like it and want to publish it, fine. Of course, I understand that you are overloaded on Bukowski, but I always want you to have first look. If, for any reasons, you don't want to, or can't, do it, please return as I only have 3 copies of the play. I'll try City Lights. Financially it has really helped to have 2 U.S. publishers, especially in the European market. I think rather than let *Barfly* lay fallow, I should get it out. Yes, I suppose there are dangers of overexposure but then I think I write too much for one publisher to keep up with me, and from a different viewpoint it might not be fair to plow half of it under. Or so I'd like to think.

So lemme know whatcha think . . .

[To Carl Weissner]
May 21, 1979, drinking zinfandel, 1975, via Louis M. Martini, St. Helena, Napa County . . .

Thanks for yours. Well, *The Rats of Thirst* has been changed back to the original title, *Barfly*. Barbet says this more fits the motion picture world, and he knows more about that than I do. Of course, I am more literary and prefer *The Rats* but since Barbet is on the run for money he has enough troubles without me fighting him about it. I got ten thousand dollars for writing the damn thing and there's more to come when and if it gets into shooting and then the 5%, and so I am sitting here (as you know) a long ways from the days of starvation but there still remains enough madness and confusion to carry me through. I was born a misfit and remain so. Simple acts of life that most men can carry off without a thought can and do befuddle me. Luckily I have gotten paid for being an ass, and only the angels can bring one that. [★ ★ ★]

Martin has some guy Fonzi (?) offering a great movie contract for some of the Sparrow books . . . the contract is so good it's almost frightening. It seems a long time back since I was freezing in that $1.25 a week paper shack in Atlanta, starving and waving at an overhanging electric light cord (shredded) with my hand, seeing how close I could come . . . I might be back there yet.

Shit, look, I just bought a new 1979 BMW, sunroof and all the bits, $16,000 cash. The tax accountant says I can get a 52% tax write-off, which means instead of giving the 16 grand to Sam I only give him 8 and I got me a new car. No, it doesn't *quite* work that way, but almost. The idea is to keep yourself down from the upper tax brackets one way or another and if you put all the money in the bank and don't come up with tax write-offs the damn govt. just walks in and takes almost all of it, and so they force you to spend, they force you into a different life style, and I guess that can harm the writing but if I'm a good enough writer I can overcome that; if I'm not a good enough writer then I'm going to get what I've got coming to me. o.k.

I guess the d.a. [Los Angeles District Attorney] is worried about the pocketbook because it reaches more people at a smaller price, and it's nice to be accused of "obscenity" and "advocating violence." it puts me in the same camp as a lot of immortals. not that I am concerned with being immortal, only that there were some good word-throwers among them.

for you, I imagine translating can really be hell because one thing it does is keep your energy from getting at and doing your own work but it also keeps you out of the factories and/or teaching literature at some fucking university with the girls in the front rows flashing their thighs at you for grades. and what is really important, I think about the ways you can *improve* on these writers (including me) by putting them into German; part of your personality does enter and that's a creative act, my friend.

thanks for letting me know all the things, and as always luck and love to Voltrout and Mike, and to you too, from Linda Lee and me. Christ, we've just found a small tree and it's bearing apples! and the roses are pounding into the sky, it's dangerous and beautiful, and there's no gasoline in California and we wait in two hour long lines in our cars listening to rock music, drinking beer, getting angry and shooting and knifing each other. this Rome is falling, tottering, insipid. I don't care; if anybody's got it coming, we have.

[To John Martin]
May 31, 1979

I got the 2nd printing of *Women* today. Looks fine, thanks. People keep commenting on what a good job Barbara did on the cover. [* * *]

Well, the apricot tree is full and there's even a little apple tree going at it, and the horses are going well, and Linda and I are not fighting.

[To John Martin]
June 10, 1979

I know you have the movie on your mind right now. That's fine. But, meanwhile, here's more poems, good or bad.

I know you do a lot of work on the side to protect my ass, to see that I don't get burned, and I want you to know that I'm aware of that and grateful for that.

Don't worry, I'll never be as rich as you are; you are running an industry; I am a member of this particular asylum, you know.

[To William Packard]
June ten 1 nine 7 nine

[* * *] took some mushrooms earlier that I paid $25 for, hardly anything. Thomas Hardy. Thomas Mann. You know, you can have most of the Tommies. And a lot of the Edgars too. you know somebody I think of now and then: Knut Hamsun. he ground it out, fat novels and thin, mostly fat, and when the fat ones hold up, that's the real score. I never read anything of his that he failed at. there are men who are simply fuck-

ing landscapes – like Sibelius. I got my new 1979 MGM[*sic*] and on the way to the track I often slip in a little Sibelius and listen to him over the front and back speakers, sun roof open, I get ready for the tote board, I play the horses like most men play chess and I usually win, it helps the writing and it helps the appetite and it's nice to have decent pocket money so Linda Lee and I can eat at Musso's and stock up on good German riesling, yes. (Havemeyer 1977 Berich Bernkastel.)

in the mornings, hungover, I lay with my ass up to the sun in a big yard full of fruit trees and berries and I let the others worry about my soul. that's their job; my job is to get along with my 17 private and personal gods and so far we are all voting for the same thing, though what it is we are not too sure of. [★ ★ ★]

[To John Martin]
June 18, 1979

We'll just have to forget about "the image." I never hide anything.

The car is a 1979 black BMW, sun roof and all. 320I. (52% tax write-off.) [★ ★ ★]

[To Carl Weissner]
July 14, 1979

Actually, I am glad the Jan. tour has been called off. When I think of freezing my bunghole and reading 5 times in one week I don't miss it. If I were alone I would never have said "yes" to it. Linda is so crazy for travel I was doing it for her. And you know the first rule: never do anything for anybody else. So I'm glad it's called off. [★ ★ ★]

I seem to be writing only poems now, ten to twenty a week, they seem to be all right, the *New York Quarterly* and *Wormwood* taking some and not returning the rest – yet. The *Quarterly* is going to publish a "craft interview" with Bukowski in issue #27, I think. I tell 'em my craft is to get drunk and write, mostly after the racetrack. I more or less tell them to jam it, but they don't seem to mind. I think the editor is partial to crazies. o.k. [★ ★ ★]

A couple of movie deals swinging in the wind. If one of them goes through I'll have to see my tax man and figure out how to spend it so the U.S. tax man doesn't get most of it. Like I get 52% off on the old (1979) black BMW. Now I may have to get the house painted and put in a jacuzzi. First, let's see. You know, writing is a strange thing: IT CAN STOP. So I'm always precautionary, figuring out how I can pull it out if the roof falls in. I can see myself in a tiny room sucking on a beercan and staring [?starting] all over again. It would make a good story. As always, there's no rest in my mind, no matter what kind of life it is. The cemetery is the best bet on the board; all we do is stall that number off as long as we can. I'd like to hang around a bit longer, I still love the sound of this typer, the drink to my left, the cigarette to the right, the radio sending me music that is centuries old.

The horses have been lucky lately. Only a week left and the track closes. Don't know what I'll do then. Probably sleep all day. Sometimes I get this urge to go to bed for a week and stay there. I used to do it. It's great. When you get up you are powerful as a polar bear and everything looks great and different. It lasts about 2 days. Then it's back to shit in the streets and in the heart and in the stratosphere.

Linda sends love to all and wants to know if there is anything we can mail you folks from good old Southern California? An oil well? The Queen Mary?

[To William Packard]
July ending, one97nine

Here's a few more and the plan is now to go into prose a bit; I slide back and forth between those two prosties, prose und poem, I don't know why more people don't give themselves relief like that.

Lucked it again, passed up reading poetry with 21 American poets, 21 Italians, in some town over there. I mean, when you get at least 42 poets reading, somebody is going to get sick, and they did (the audience, I mean). One long time famous American poet began his chanting and got vegetables in the face when he wasn't quite ready to eat them. I'm told the others fared as badly. Here in America the poet simply gets away with reading too much bad and contrived shit and the audience is used to swallowing it. It's about time somebody told these that the game is up. The sad thing is that most (but not all) poets who gain some fame begin with some bombast, originality, guts, then quickly accept their role, become teachers, leaders, lookers into mirrors. I don't understand why they don't understand that to remain alive is more difficult than to be alive in the first place.

wait. I'm out of wine. have to go downstairs. ain't that something? I have a stairway to go down. And I never forget it, each time. stairway. I am doing it, going down it, good luck, refrigerator there, open it, chilled gong-high glory in bottle, bravo, but just a moment of it, anything can happen. now wait . . . I'm back, I get letters from the young. some say I've saved their lives. it's not so. if it were, I wouldn't be interested . . . how do you do it? they ask. what can I do? what did you do? I basket the letters. I can't help them because I don't know.

what I did, what I do wouldn't help them. I still need help. I am as confused as I was when it began. nothing has been solved.

my woman is good, she is a good one but I tell her, you must go talk to your friends. she says, is it another woman? and I tell her, no. but women need to be set free into space now and then or they'll claw you to death. they don't mean to. but they do.

we are all too precious. we are all too terribly precious. and we are all looking for the hero (or the heroine) and there just aren't any. I like a cat asleep upon the rug. That's best. If you can have a cat and you can have a rug. that's best. and one more drink . . .

[To John Martin]
August 2, 1979

[* * *] Behind on a lot of standard paper work here; have to get it done; it ain't poetic but if you don't do it, they send in the troops. I am fighting against computer errors from the Authorities right now. It's amazing: you write them back a factual truth and the machine is off-feed and it spits it all out and says, no, no, no. And that's all they go by. Almost every day, besides some demented fan mail, I get some sort of letter claiming that I owe something for something that I never purchased, like 3 grey-hounds and a washing machine propelled by wild goldfish. . . .

Weissner's translations were published as Western Avenue: Gedichte aus über 20 Jahren 1955–1977 *by Zweitausendeins, Frankfurt.*

[To Carl Weissner]
August 2, 1979

yes, all the people who see *Western Ave.* marvel at it, and I know the translation is epic and gutsy. see ya ended with Bogart, you romantic. good. quite. I know you ought to win the war of awards, but "ought to" and politics are different things.

on the Italian thing, I just looked at the list of 21 American poets and knew it was a puke situation — little flamboyant sweeties who love to croon into the mike. the vanity of these types is only exceeded by their lack of talent.

over here, still going upstairs with the wine and typing out poems almost every night. the disease appears to be permanent. After *Women, Shakespeare*, and *Barfly*, I just fall back onto and into the poem like a champagne bath. on *Barfly*, Schroeder appears to be reeling in a backer and also is considering using this fellow Woods who was the only compelling force in a film which failed for me: *The Onion Field*. The schedule is that we get drunk with him and attempt to make him over into a Chinaski. no easy thing. the fellow talks very fast, seems desperate enough but not tired enough. we could re-do him a bit. I think that *Barfly*, properly done, should shake some asses in the theater seats. I don't trust Hollywood, of course, but this thing ain't exactly Hollywood . . . meanwhile, some of the Italians came by (Di Fonzi and crew) and we got drunk with them, and they ain't hardly Hollywood either, so I'm not dead yet. but so far there's been more talk than money. [* * *]

[To John Martin]
August 18, 1979

This is 60 buck portable so in case I ever go to Europe I'll have something to escape to besides the bottle. But it just doesn't have the soul of the old . . . Olympia, which is still being fixed. Delay, of course. Yes, nobody can do anything . . . poets can't write poetry, cabbies can't drive, so on . . . Got car out of garage . . . 2 day wait . . . drove one block, had to take it back in again . . . The people are bothered with *nerves*, they don't want to do what they are doing but they don't want to starve either so they just *pretend* to be doing something, but they can only back off from it because it's just rote and dizziness, they want the money without the effort. The thing has even spread into professional sports. The artistry has gone out of everything; it's all being done on a very dull and low level. The tax man fucks up, the waitress fucks up, the cop shoots the wrong guy . . . on and on it goes. I don't mind so much what they do, humanity has hardly been one of my loves, but when what they do gets in the way of my existence, when I have to take hours and days to straighten out *their* errors and malfunctions, *then* what *I* am trying to do becomes affected and I begin to fail somewhat because they fail entirely, and we are all stuck in the same bog. o.k.

I hear through the vine that Galiano has already shot *Rape Rape*, that he is getting Polanski (Roman the child-fucker) ready to direct another . . . meanwhile, no monies, not even option money. contract signed for $44,000. sometimes I feel like getting an m.g. and walking into an office and gunning these bastards down, and within my nature I am perfectly capable of doing that. Nothing miffs me like lying and cheating and outright stealing, plus indifference and silence about matters . . .

[* * *] In the future the money won't be like this because now (if it comes) it comes off of a mass of work already published and they have just about caught up with us. [* * *]

[To John Martin]
September 7, 1979

Yes, the world's at war and they don't know it. You're right. And it can get irritating at times when they scratch the back of their necks and get ready to pick the best bowling ball. Not that a person shouldn't enjoy himself when his house is burning down, it's only what they select for enjoyment that (which) puzzles me. So? Well, it's like Schopenhauer basically said in a certain place: I certainly seem to suffer like a son of a bitch most of the time, living among them and this, but, for it all, I have one thing that I am glad for and that is that I am not them. . . .

I've walked up the railroad tracks and I'm still walking up them. The essence doesn't change. There are still things to be handled; there will always be things to be handled. Nobody ever gets caught up and finished on what there is to do. And even if you do, for a moment, feel a central peace, there is always somebody walking behind you with a switchblade. The philosophers of the centuries have probably said the same thing but in, and with, such an involuted and private and dead language that they themselves were part of the failure they were speaking of.

Women are strange, they are positive: they want to build swimming pools while you wonder who the hell and how the hell the water bill is going to be paid? They are thinking about next Saturday night while you are thinking about 3 years from now, *if* you are here. Somebody has to be the wolf, somebody has to be the hunting dog, somebody has to drill the 3 and 2 pitch between first and second. When you slow down a step, the good times are over. Good times? There were never good times. There were bad times and times not as bad. People like to talk about the Brotherhood of Man. Two types: those who have nothing and would like a Brotherhood because they *think* that would bring them something; and those who have everything (materially) and speak of the Brotherhood of Man as *now* because they think it's working for them at the moment.

As far as relaxing goes in the midstream of the dangerous tempo, I've done it. I got drunk for ten years without doing anything. Anybody can be a slob but to be a deliberate slob takes some doing, well, at least a minor inventiveness.

There is something about these now, they simply don't have the hardness and/or the honor of those who grew up in the 30's. Even their body movements, their speech is putty-soft and irreverent to the Fact. And the Fact is what occurs when you face something head-on. I once spoke of the Absence of the Hero, that was sad enough. I now speak of the absence of a human among humans, one face in a crowd of no-faces. Now it's feces and a flavescent flatulence. Nobody scares me anymore; a cop pulls me over, gets off his bike, he has a valentine ass and an english toffee face; no matter if he pulls his gun and blasts my brains out, he can't even do it with style and aplomb, he's just a mechanism, a test-tube baby, doing his thing to protect a neurotic wife playing with cheap coke in a housing development in Dijo Valley.

Sometimes there's a small chance, you can see it for a moment in the face of a waitress in a cheap cafe, an old waitress, beaten, nowhere to go, there is some truth in that face, which is more than there is in the truth of the face of your landlord or your president. Of course, she can't speak to you and you can't speak to her. Words would mutilate, words have too long been used the wrong way. You put in your order and wait. Sometimes you see it in the face of a boxer, a prize fighter, sometimes in the face of an old newsboy. But you don't see it too often, and you see it less and less.

So, this isn't really a letter and it isn't really a poem; it's good not to fit the form, always. The two bottles of wine have been good, and sleep is good too, lately I've gone toward sleep like I've gone towards drunkenness. Here's the last glass. Let me pick it up, drink it. It's gone. I light the last cigarette, and once again I think of my boy John Dillinger. Now look, you see, I'm going to piss and then to sleep it off . . .

your boy, Henry

[To John Martin]
September 17, 1979

Yes, it goes on and on . . .

I was in a health food store with Linda the other day and there were 3 or 4 lines snaking around and the clerks at the counter were chatting limply with the customers at hand and the customers at hand were chatting limply with the clerks, and even those others waiting didn't sense that time was being mutilated, that silliness and ineptness were dripping from the walls. There was no fire or motion anywhere. And it just wasn't a physical stagnation, you could sense their wilted cottonball spirits . . . zeroes giving off horrifying death-rays.

I told Linda, "I'll bet John Martin and I would have these lines worked down and away in no time at all."

"Sure you would," she said, "but you see, people just aren't like that nowadays."

oh, my god. . . . [★ ★ ★]

[To Carl Weissner]
September 17, 1979

The *ecce homo* book by George Grosz was an astonishing birthday gift. You certainly know my taste. Some of this man's work reminds me of my own short stories. It is some book and one that can be looked at over and over again. But, Carl, you needn't remember my birthday, you are doing too many things at once, take it easy. [★ ★ ★]

Smog and heat have descended; this area usually all right, fairly smog-free but the Santa Ana winds blew it in from the inner city and we've had it for two days . . . Linda downstairs looking at an anti-war movie, *Coming Home*. I don't bother with those. I don't think any artist is being daring and original when they state that War is Bad. That takes as much courage as hitting grandma behind the neck with a two-by-four. [★ ★ ★]

[To Gerald Locklin]
September 19, 1979

[★ ★ ★] I am honored that you are laying the *Piano* on some of your students for a week. The idea, of course, might be to let them know that writing needn't be hard work; the hard work is getting out of bed in the morning or at noon; the hard work is looking at people's faces in long supermarket lines; the hard work is working for somebody else who is making money using your life's hours and years. The typing comes easy, especially with the chilled wine in the thermos to the left of the machine. [★ ★ ★]

[To Hank Malone]
October 15, 1979

So you're still in Highland Park with Sharon – she seemed a good one, might do you well to stick around. I've been with one almost 3 years, basically good sort, although some of her ideas on the Hereafter and her particular god seem to me to be pretty assy, her other qualities seem to overcome most of that. She's the "Sara" of the novel *Women*. Linda Lee, actually. [★ ★ ★]

No, I didn't vomit on national tv in France. I just got stinking drunk, said a few things and walked off, pulled my knife on a security guard. Actually it was good luck. All of the newspapers in France gave it a good write-up except one. It went over good with the people of the streets. Went to Nice next day, was sitting getting drunk with Linda Lee at outside table and 6 French waiters waved, then walked up in a line, stood and bowed. I write better of the incident in a book due out in November via City Lights, *Shakespeare Never Did This*, all about the European trip. Actually, it's two European trips jammed into one with photos. I think it might be lively writing.

Finished a screenplay called *Barfly* for Barbet Schroeder and he claims he's going to do it, although at the moment he's only pulled in $200,000 for production and it takes maybe 5 times that but he's good at that sort of thing. Meanwhile, *Women* and *Factotum* have a good chance to become movies. Di Fonzi of Italy says he is going to produce it here in America (them) and he seems to mean it. So it's contract time and lawyers, all that shit. I drink with strange people now, including James Woods of *Holocaust* and *The Onion Field*. He wants to be the Chinaski of *Barfly* and I think he's a good actor . . . Meanwhile, I still write 15 poems a week. I've got this room upstairs overlooking the harbor and I drink 2 or 3 bottles of wine and tap it out. *NYQ* just accepted 12 poems. So I'm not finished yet . . .

Just back from Vancouver. Read to 680 at Viking Inn, standing room only. Drank before reading and 4 bottles of red wine during. Got back to hotel, fell and cracked my head open real damn good on the heater. Probably my best poem of the night. [★ ★ ★]

[To John Martin]
October 25, 1979

It takes about two weeks to get over one of those readings. I don't understand how the poets can go on reading, some of them giving two or three readings a month . . . Yes, I know how they can do it: vanity. And also, lack of energy: when they read they sound as if they were lisping into teacups.

Back at the track, trying to forget all that nonsense. I play the horses like the average man plays chess or maybe like an extra average man plays chess. I know all the traps, bad plays, panic plays. I've only had time to attend the meet 6 days, won 5, lost one day. I bet moderately. I've averaged about $90 profit a day. I suppose if I were a desperate man playing for the rent and the baby food I would lose. But going to the track, making my bets, following my knowledge, this teaches me *movement*. A cutting through the fog. I can understand why Hemingway went to the bullfights. There is death at the track too and there is life and sometimes victory. All the women I have known have been incensed with my horseplaying. They think it is very foolish and when they attend the races with me they become angry because I usually win and they usually lose. The problem is that they don't put any effort into the game, they are listless and distracted. And it's strange that most of them believe in some kind of God. That doesn't take any effort either. At the track one must overcome a 15 percent take.

Well, it's been about 20 years since my first book, *Flower, Fist and Bestial Wail* was published when I was 40. I think it's been a good twenty years of creation and I think it's still coming. And even if it should stop now, I'd feel particularly lucky. And I was lucky when the Sparrow came by and you printed my stuff when it wasn't particularly *literary*, you know what I mean. I'm sure you've heard plenty about it from some quarters. So it's been a good show. Let them rage, let them weep, let them bitch. o.k.

Poems enclosed.

[To William Packard]
October 25, 1979

Back from Canada. Vancouver. Hall held 500. 680 drunks showed up. We played classical music over the speakers. I had a bit to drink in the afternoon, then came out and threw it at them. I drank 3 bottles of red wine during the reading. You know, if I can't be entertained I'm not going to entertain them.

I fooled them again. Party afterwards, more booze. I danced, kept falling down. I make an excellent fool; in the days of the kings I never would have been unemployed.

I don't remember much. But I got the money. 1000 plus air and expenses. Linda says they got me back to the hotel and into the elevator and I demanded another bottle. After they left I staggered about the room, finally fell and cracked my head open against the radiator. Great gash in skull. Blood everywhere. It looked like a murder sex orgy had been in that room. Linda cleaned it up in the morning. Nice town, Vancouver. I still can't comb my hair. But great part happening now. Picking at this long scab. Really living. Poems enclosed.

[To Carl Weissner]
November 9, 1979

[* * *] Back from Canadian reading. Took Linda. Have video tapes of the thing in color, runs about two hours. Saw it a couple nights back. Not bad. Much fighting with the audience. New poems. Dirty stuff and the other kind. Drank before the reading and 3 bottles of red wine during but read the poems out. Dumb party afterwards. I fell down several times while dancing. They got me on the elevator back at the hotel and I kept hollering for another bottle. Poor Linda. Afterwards in hotel room, kept falling. Finally fell against the radiator and cracked a 6 inch gash in skull. Blood everywhere. Hell of a trip. [* * *] Nice Canadian people who set up reading, though. Not poet types at all. All in all, a good show.

Thanks for sending rundowns on monies. Have rec. all. All is well. Mortgage half paid for. I figure if I get this place paid I can make a stand here after the talent diminishes and they start closing in. It's a great place, Carl. I wish your gang were here in that downstairs bedroom. You'd all like the harbor, and the people. San Pedro and Mannheim are my two favorite places. [* * *]

[To William Packard]
November 27, 1979

Well, we all approach the dreaded season. I've been climbing up this Christmas–Happy New Year cross for some time now, and it doesn't get any better. One New Year's I just went to bed and cut the lights and pulled up the covers and stayed there, phone off the hook and not drinking. It was my happiest New Year.

Won 9 races in a row the other day, that's 9 firsts, and that's some going you know, none of them favorites, On some days there is total control, you drive the freeways better, you do everything better. Then the other days arrive when you even fear the check-out girl in the supermarket.

Too many nights now with movie people who talk about camera angles, and producer directors who go to baseball games with Jack Nicholson, kissing his ass, trying to get him to act in their movies when they should really be kissing the ass of his agent. Rich girls laying on the backs of sofas with nothing to do. All very dangerous and swampland territory. I suppose they must be better people than I make them but I can only see that they drink from morning to night, sleep four in a bed, are always on the telephone or preparing food. It's good to get back here with my two cars and Linda Lee and to turn on the radio and drink the petite sirah and inhale the quiet walls.

seasons gratings,

[To A. D. Winans]
December 29, 1979

I don't see how you've stood the little mag game as long as you have, but no, I can't read, I don't know which is worse, that Frisco gang or the so-called New York School. [* * *]

It's not true, as per rumor, that I have purchased a sports car; it's a 1979 BMW and now it is in my poems instead of the 69 Volks. About buying a house, it's not that easy; I've got a mortgage around my neck. Both investments were made to help avoid some of the tax bite out of European royalties. Here in America, if you don't lay the money off, they take it. I offer no excuses for buying a car or living in a house. Although some may take this as a sign that I am losing my soul, most of these same have been saying for years that I am losing, have lost, my soul. If these would pay as much heed to their typewriters as they did to my soul (or lack of) they might (?) get some work done. [* * *]

[To John Martin]
December 29, 1979

There won't be any poems for a little while. It won't mean I've died. Barbet laying some more money on me and I'm going to re-work *Barfly* a bit. It shouldn't take too long.

We had one large producer willing to make *Barfly* into a major motion picture. Only one catch – he wanted to use Chris Christoferson [*sic*] as Chinaski, and in the part where Chinaski comes back to the room and lays in the dark listing to classical music, he wants Chris Chris to break out his guitar and start singing. We told him, no.

1980. It's been a long war. We're rushing in fresh troops. Enemy still everywhere.

Happy new 365,

your boy, Henry

• 1980 •

[To John Martin]
June 14, 1980

There have been too many visitors and now Linda tells me that "mother" is coming soon. I am curious as to why people visit each other when there is hardly time to do the singular and necessary things, and one of the most necessary things is to do all the shit and trivial things to keep the gross and mindless forces from murdering you, and the other necessary thing to do is to do absolutely nothing, glorious spaces away from all things – it's kind of an easy breathing and if you don't get that no matter what else you do nothing can take form. But people don't seem to need this last. They need "togetherness," this legendary humanity of triviality; they need to sit in chairs and chatter away the hours. I feel uncomfortable doing this; I feel like a turd doing this; I feel violated; worse than this, I feel bad. And I know that the only way to shake them is to act like a "prick." So, most of the time I am ingested and the visitors leave fulfilled. Where do they get all this time to wallow about in and to piss away? To me, each minute is a guarantee against loss; I've had hours, years murdered working for other men for their benefit. Don't *these* have this background? Has it always been a welfare, roll-down the hill blind yawn? I mean, what's there to *say* in a room together? What's there to do? So they want to *go* somewhere. They are interested in things. We go. What a burning of garbage. I don't need movies, jazz clubs, fish shows. "How can you be a writer?" one of my women once asked me, "you're not interested in anything."

Why must I like what they like? Does this make me inhuman? And if I am inhuman why must they try to humanize me? Where are *my* rights? Must I always act like a "prick" in order to obtain them (my rights)? Every now and then when one of them overencroaches (that's a beautiful word) I've had to say "enough" and they always leave wounded as if the guilt were mine, as if there were something that I lacked. I never knock on doors. What do they want with me? And each one that is gotten rid of is replaced by another. The world is full of the lonely and the lonely are full of poison. I have never been lonely. One of the finest things for me in all my life has been to close a door and to be in a room without anybody else about.

After this long string of visitors I actually became ill – chills, fever, my legs weakened, I could hardly walk. it was them, too much of them. I was sick for a god damned week. I'm not trying to act like a precious and delicate soul, John. One of my X-Women got it best – Stella – she drank scotch through her nostrils and could smoke up a room with her Pall Malls in 30 minutes but she knew something, she said, "Don't people *realize* you're a fucking *recluse*?"

That's one of the best things I like about our relationship: you leave me alone and I leave you alone and we do what we have to do. I regret very much that I bothered you while Linda was on her night-run trip. This was non-professional and weak; the next time there is trouble I will concur with the inside of my own dome. You were helpful then, thanks, but in the future it will not be needed. Things go in waves, fall up and down, but then we get past that and into our own clear. That's good, that way. But if Barbara ever starts swinging from the vines, feel free to call. I owe you one, and I have this vast backlog from the chamber of horrors that might make you laugh when you need to laugh. o.k.

Henry Miller. I didn't feel much when he went because I've been expecting it. What I liked is that when he was going he went to paint and what I've seen of his things are very good, warm, hot color. Not many lives like his. In his writing, he did the thing like that, when nobody else was going it, doing it. He cracked the hard black walnut. I always had trouble reading him because he would leave off into this Star-Trek contemplation sperm-jizz babble but it made the good parts better when you finally got to them, but frankly, I usually gave up most of the time. Lawrence was different, he was solid all the way through but Miller was more modern, less artsy, until he got into his Star-Trek babbling. I think a problem Miller caused (and it's not his fault) is that when he hustled and pushed his stuff (early) he has made others think that's the way it is done, so now we have these battalions of semi-writers knocking on doors and hustling and proclaiming their genius because they have been "undiscovered" and that the very fact of non-discovery makes them sure of their genius because "the world is not ready for them yet."

For most of them the world will never be ready; they don't know how to write, they are simply not touched by the grace of the word or the way.

Not those I have met or read. I hope there are others. We need them. It's pretty fallow, around. But even like those who come around with their guitars, I've found that the least talented scream the loudest, are the most abusive and the most self-assured. They've slept on my couches and puked on my rugs and drank my drinks and they have told me, continuously, of their greatness. I'm not a publisher of songs or poems or novels and/or short stories. The battlefield has an address; to beg of friends or girlfriends or others is masturbation against the sky. Yes, I'm drinking very much wine tonight and I guess I'm dizzied with the visitors. Writers, please save me from the writers; the conversation of the Alvarado street whores was much more interesting, and more original.

Don't worry about the novel.[1] Let me do that. If it comes, it comes. I have a feeling that it will. Next thing I need is an outline so I won't write it and then find back in chapter 9 I left out a scene that was the best of them all. Besides, by cracking [sic] out poems in between, it tightens the skin of the work to come. I made a mistake in letting it out that I am possibly into novel #4. There's this one fellow I am affiliated with on another score and when he phones the first thing he asks is, "How is the novel coming?" You know, this novel is not a task, it is not something to be done. It's between me and me, and that's simple enough.

Henry Miller. A damn good soul. He liked Céline like I like Céline. Like I told Neeli Cherry, "the secret is in the line." And I meant one line at a time. Lines containing factories and a shoe on its side next to a beer-can in a hotel room. Everything is there, it flashes back and forth. They are not going to beat us, not even the graves. The joke is ours; we pass through in high style; there's nothing that they can do with us.

---

[1] *Ham on Rye.*

> *Joe Stapen in 1980 was, in his own words, "a recently divorced psychiatrist in Denver who enjoyed poetry but came late to Bukowski."*

[To Joe Stapen]

December 28, 1980

[* * *] I went to a madhouse once, as visitor, and remember walking about the grounds laughing with my girlfriend, we couldn't stop, I think it was because we sensed that we could be crazy, especially me. I can't describe the mood – it was just joyous being crazy and not being bothered about it, and I picked a flower and held it high in the air and waved to people and we couldn't stop laughing, waving and laughing as the faces stared back sedately. But getting inside, seeing the patients, it got strange, dark-hued, it got flat, it seemed stale, drab and senseless. The boys and girls were comfortable, just like blocks of wood. Nobody was flying over the cuckoo's nest, they were sitting in it. Of course, maybe the violent ward was more entertaining. I didn't try for it. Then I met one of my readers there. In a way, that's better than being in the New York Public library.

I get many of my letters from people in madhouses and jails and some from strange people out of them. What they say, mainly, is that I have given them a reason for going on: "Since you are so fucked-up, Bukowski, and still around, there is a chance for me." But I don't write to save people; I dislike most of them. I feel best when I am totally alone. I've tried to answer most of my letters, especially from people in the madhouses but I found that an answer just brings another letter, a longer one and a stranger one. And more and more letters come and there just isn't time to answer them, not with the racetrack and the drinking and fights with the woman and then just *writing* itself, for me, for money and for me.

Like, I don't know what to say to you. I put the words down and I forget them. Somebody once asked me what my theory of life was and I said, "Don't try." That fits the writing too. I don't try, I just type, and if I say any more than that, I'm trying.

Like right now I'm drinking this Concannon petite sirah, vintage 1976 and listening to classical music on the radio and I've got this capitalistic silly itch to shape a poem or something like that.

I wish you luck with your people and luck with yourself. Nothing, of course, has never fit right and the truly contented man is the insane one. There'll never be an out for us. Just endure if possible. Sometimes I watch my cat sleeping night and day and this teaches me more than all the books and all the past. Other times it doesn't help. Meanwhile, there's some wine, and the itch.

· 1981 ·

[To Louise Webb]
January 9, 1981

I know you think I'm a son of a bitch for not keeping closer touch, but you know how that happens – give a man a touch of fame and he's too busy watching his own ass in the mirror to remember the real beginnings.

You probably still have your emphasemia (spell?) but I always figured New Orleans was luckier for you than any other place. Whenever I saw you there I figured you belonged there rather than the other places. Jon's been gone a long time but both of us know what good things he did for both of us. [★ ★ ★]

With me, it's about the same. Still drinking, typing and playing the horses. I live in a big house now. It's not paid for but I live in it. First time I've ever had all this space. A good place to die, I guess. Finally living with a woman who isn't a whore. She's religious but most women are. Not much I can do about that. It's her business.

My luck's good in that most of my fame is in Europe. Over there I can't walk the streets. Here it's good. I can live a normal life. Especially in San Pedro. Old harbor town full of working people, Mexicans, Blacks, Yugos. My neighbors don't bother me. I have 3 cats and much ground out front. I grew some stuff last year – now it's all weeds. Got to get it cleared out. This house is screwed up. Had a handy man here, did his own plumbing and wiring. Got to pay somebody to straighten things out. Got to keep writing for the plumbing, the wiring and the mortgage. Really not that. It still feels mad and clean to sit down in front of this thing . . .

You ever come west, do visit us. phone [★ ★ ★]. We have an extra bedroom and we drink good wine. Linda knows about you. We've got one copy of *Crucifix* and one copy of *It Catches* left. We show them to people when they come by and they marvel at the artistry of the bookwork, as they should. [★ ★ ★]

[To Louise Webb]
January 20, 1981

Well, I don't have an agent . . . not in the U.S. and I don't know of any. It would be great if you could get "Four Steps" done into a movie but, my god, it's difficult. I wrote a screenplay, *Barfly*, a good year or so ago and the director who wants to do it knows many people personally – producers and the works – but no luck, and I think it's a good screenplay. I wish I could help you but I don't know anybody.

Yes, I got cooled by W.C. [Corrington] some time back, a long time back. I was broke and asked him if he might send me the letters I had written him for some archives a university wanted for $$$. I told him that he had written me that whenever I wanted the letters I could have them. He said he never recalled writing a letter like that. He told me to send him that letter and he would mail the letters back to me. I sent the letter. (I should have xeroxed it). Nothing. Silence. Well, you know . . .

About the movie people – sometimes a guy will buy an option for the rights to a work, say for a year. They will pay almost nothing for the option and then try to re-sell the work to somebody else for a profit. I shouldn't call these types "movie people," they are more like the suckerfish of the universe. Be careful of them, they will glad talk you and get your hopes up for nothing. But often if they have a good work for cheap, they can't get rid of it because they are so personally obnoxious. I'm not saying your fellow is one of these, only that he might be. [★ ★ ★]

[To John Martin]
February 4, 1981

Thanks for the rundown on the books. It's nice to see my children doing so well. It's especially strange and lucky that the old books are still moving too. I'm not partial to any of them, old or new. I like them all.

I got myself depressed on the novel when I told you I was going to re-write the whole thing. I can't do that, it's too much like working for the post office. What I will do is to re-write certain portions I didn't like or that read without verve. Then if you want to publish it you can go over it then for syntax and get a bit of the grammar and spelling but don't make it *too* smooth. If there is anything good about my writing it *is* the roughness, the quality of *not* being literary. But it's good of you to straighten out the few kinks that might just be too sloppy. My thanks, plenty.

I've done a few drawings for the proposed new book of poesy[1] but ran out of paints. I use the little tubes. Next time I go to Standard Brands I'm going to load up.

I've been a little low down lately. I can write poems no matter how I feel, good or bad. But to write prose, I can't feel bad and it's better if I feel pretty good. Things will lift soon, I'm sure.

[To John Martin]
April 16, 1981

The Linda situation will probably go into a continuance. If not, I can scramble eggs with the best of them,

Pity the poor writer, he not only attracts madwomen, he not only destroys his liver with drinking, he also has no Union (except in Hollywood) and few working rights and/or benefits. Stuck with his sickness for the word and usually having contempt for the business world he is left with nothing but to trust the others, and leaning on that, he is usually taken.

Your $250 bimonthly check which would break down into 6000 a year would probably make me eligible for food stamps. This doesn't so much reflect my ability as a writer as it does Black Sparrow's limited distribution. B.S. may print books as rare as diamonds and gain a literary reputation but not many people are buying diamonds these day, percentagewise. You probably make more on selling my works overseas (the right to publish), selling paperback rights and other similar rights, plus your cut of overseas sales than you do on paying me B.S. royalties. You can't miss.

Why an author derives no payment on the publication rights of his own creations (and other related rights) has always seemed unfair to me. This has been caused by writers being writers and not businessmen, and all the editors tell them is, "This is the way it has always been." Then the

---

1. *Dangling in the Tournefortia*.

dear little writers, as their talents dwindle, as most talents must, watch their royalties dwindle likewise, and since royalties are all they have (had) upon some distant tabulation from some distant place, they become more than bitter, end up in mental and charity wards or as suicides.

It has always been the popular concept for the writer to starve, go mad, suffer, suicide. I think it's time for the editors and publishers to starve, suffer, go mad and suicide. I think it's time the writers got fat guts and drank champagne for breakfast. I think it's time for the writers to sleep with the golden girls of kindness.

They won't, of course, they are too interested in getting the god damned word down as the world breaks down their last door. I am too. I hate this haggling. I'd rather be at Del Mar watching them break out of the gate, with the lady sunning herself at the beach and the wine getting chilled in the motel room, and the portable typer under the bed. I don't like to haggle. The publishers drove Céline mad, pissed H. Miller off. There are, were, countless others. We never get our dues but if we only got half of them we'd feel fine. One of Perkins' editors may have rearranged Thomas Wolfe but Wolfe was there to begin with. What is often called the writer's self-pity is only his tabulation of society whose honor is milk thin. Sour milk thin.

By the way, when I phone you now and then when there's a jam here, it's not that I expect advice or solace, it's only an old habit gotten out of working the factories and the p.o. and all the other places, a subconscious calling in *sick*, meaning I won't be able to work for a while. It seems ingrained. It's a mistake. A good man is best when he works out of jams alone. 0-and-two doesn't mean crap. You can crack the next one over the wall. I'm back at the plate.

[To Al Fogel]
April 22, 1981

Hardly anybody makes it at the track – besides the plus 15% take other things conspire – horses in trouble, fuckers fail to break out of gate, jock is drunk or having trouble with his whore, all the dismal x-factors that can break the best of horse-playing souls and minds in half.

I've gotten hot, I've averaged a string of $100 days just betting ten win on one horse each race and I've gone along like that for 3 or 4 weeks in a row and then, bingo, it doesn't hold, I'll lose $15 or I'll win $15 or the day will come when I'll only cash one ticket.

And that 30 minute wait between races can make anybody sick in the head – surrounded by dullards talking out loud about nothing they don't know. These lonely-hearts gather at racetracks because nobody can stand them anywhere else. [★ ★ ★]

I guess I go to the track because it's like getting in the ring and slugging it out with some son of a bitch. Something is learned but I'm not exactly sure what it is. I guess it beats growing a patch of gladiolus. Maybe. And to go to a track on a Saturday, Sunday, holiday, opening or closing day just shows how close to suicide all of us are.

Gerald Locklin is a college teacher and a prolific author of books of poetry from small presses.

[To Gerald Locklin]
Augy two, 1981

Hello Lock:

You've got to know, every time I come over those bridges to Long Beach and I'm with Linda Lee (we're on a part-time basis: she needs to *expand*) I start in:

"Hey, maybe we're gonna see Locklin, maybe he's standing in front of some bar."

"You gonna start that again?"

"Maybe when we go to the Glider Inn we'll see him sitting at some table drinking beer with some whore."

"I'm sure we will," says L.L.

I stick my head out the window and yell: "*Hey, Lock!*" . . .

I like San Pedro. It's a good place to hide, close to Hollywood Park, Los Alamitos. You're not going to find a bevy of poets sipping espresso anywhere along Pacific and/or Gaffey. There are some drawbacks: not a decent eating place in town and the liquor stores often close at 9:30 p.m. But since I buy by the case and have 3 or 4 bottles hidden around, I'm always all right. There's a sense of relaxation and easiness around here that you don't find in too many places. I like it.

The films, yes, mainly the Ferreri (spell?) I'd like to see. Gazzara can act and he's got good eyes. We'll see . . . I've met any number of movie people, mainly through Barbet Schroeder, cameramen, directors. mostly the European crowd, who I think get film down closer to where actuality is, except now and then they come on with some so called avant-garde stuff which I remember seeing some 40 years ago in the Art Movies in New York City . . . On the Godard subtitles: I can't speak French and I was surprised that he gave me credit. What happened is that a Frenchman translated the script into English and then I took the English script and Americanized that. But, on the other hand, Godard used one of my poems for a movie scene and I don't get credit for that, except one night we were drinking and he handed me this batch of francs, so that is cash, not credit, o.k.

There have been some cameras around looking at me and I'm not exactly sure what this has to do with creation, except that they are poking at what is left of the Chinaski soul. It's not good stuff but when I get drunk enough I don't mind. Then I can talk, then I can say things. But too much exposure is death, so I knock off a good 50% of it, and soon may stop it all. Recently turned down $2,000 to give a poetry reading because my gut is turning from this hanging from a limb and being poked at. You put a piece of paper in the machine and you type something on it. That's the essence; all the other crap is the bleed, and when they bleed you long enough and you sit down to that sheet of paper and nothing comes out, the old yea-sayers will be the first to leave. So it's best to leave them first and to get back to the mechanics of doing. Horses, booze and the typer. Anything that gets in the way of that is deathly, including women, and *especially* including women. The longer I manage to stay away from women the better I feel. Last night at the quarter horses I'm on the 2nd deck when I see this redhead with the ass and tits that I used to know, all that red hair in long fire, I see her walking up to a betting window alone. I run downstairs and bet the remainder of the night on the first floor. No more: that sticky web of madness is for the more hardy.

Besides, she was not a nice person.

Wormie [*Wormwood Review*]? Well, to me it's the only lit mag. I mean, when I get a copy I can go right to the crapper and read it while I'm shitting and I can jump into the tub or into bed and read it. I don't have any trouble with most of the poems and when I'm finished I want more. I can't say that about any other mag. When I read them I get a headache, I get sleepy, I can't turn the pages, I can't believe the stuff they get off with, 19th century posing as the poet, stuff that is so terrible that it is unbelievable, it's like a joke that doesn't work, again and again, and they keep telling it over and over. Malone has the editor's eye, that's all there is to it ... The *New York Quarterly* had a great format, and about 40 percent on the poems but they are in the process of folding even though they tell me it's not true. All I know is that it's been a couple of years since they've come out and that they're sitting on 25 or 30 of my accepted poems, but I'll live, I'll write some more.

New York City? I could only last 3 months there. It's a hard place to be without money and when you don't know the territory and you don't have a trade. That was 1944 or 1945, so maybe it's a nice place now, only I'm not going to try it.

Politics? Politics are just like women: get into them seriously and you're going to come out looking like an earthworm stepped on by a longshoreman's boot.

Well, I've got an American Express card, a Visa and a BMW but I still write, and writing has always been a pleasure to me, a non-work item, it's as easy as drinking so I usually do them both together. I hear from other writers how *hard* it is to write and if it were that god damned hard for me I'd try something different. I had my longest writer's block last month – 7 days, and most of it was caused by *people* getting in between me and the machine. Martin of Black Sparrow told me, "I've got so many of your poems on backlog that if you died today I could bring out 5 or 6 more books and all of them would be good." Of course, he's a fan. Maybe only 3 of them would be good.

I've turned down several free trips to Italy, France, Spain. That's just more *interviews*, Gerald. I'm about on page 240 on *Ham On Rye* (novel) which means it's just about done. Then a bit of re-write and then the 2 year wait for publication. That's all right. It was just 1970 that I quit the post office, and it's been a good fast glorious bang bang, and if I die right now I will have known that it was a real good cheap thrill.

There might be some new good writers around. I hope so. But I no longer read books. I read the newspaper, the race results, boxing matches. I've got *on* tv, pretty bad. I look forward to the Hearns-Leonard fight. Notice I've reversed the order of the names and also look for the fight to end that way. Duran was just a fat man. When Hearns hits Leonard, L. is going to get swatted by a lean thin man with a mule's hoof at the end of his glove. Leonard's got guts though and style. Whoever wins is really going to have to earn it.

rivers of good wine to you,

[To Gerald Locklin]
Augie what 8? 1891 [August 8, 1981]

Well, you know, the ladies, when they start asking for "air" I give it to them. I am one of these strange fuckers who finds great pleasure in being alone. I also find pleasure the other way. So, which ever way it goes, I'm functional.

I've really liked some of your poems where you have taken this problem by the horns, er tits, and with humor, style and courage – have put it where it is. Neither of us hate women. We just don't like to be bluffed out of a poker game . . . [★ ★ ★]

[To Joe Stapen]
Augie, what? ate, 1981

Well, now you can stand up in that class and holler "Bukowski" but it isn't going to do any good. The fix is in. The poetry fix is centuries old, that's why the form is practically lifeless.

I was invited up there[1] for a two week stretch to do something or other to the students or for the students. One of the lady teacher poets, from New York, I believe wrote me and invited me up.

I wrote her back thanks but that I couldn't do that sort of thing.

Then I got a letter from Ginsberg inviting me up. I sent back the same message.

Joe, you know when I don't come up when a woman calls I'm not going to come up when something else calls.

I've seen it happen again and again. Somebody starts writing poetry, they get some renown and they end up teaching others how to write poetry. They begin by railing against society and then end up on the same power trip.

How can I tell anybody how to write? Most of the time when I sit down at this machine I don't know what the fuck's coming out. And to bring poetry to people, to try to show them what it is, that's not needed. If the poetry is good enough and strong enough they are going to find it.

---

1. I.e., to the Naropa Institute.

The fry cook at your local cafe is going to be talking to the dishwasher about it.

We don't need poetry writing seminars, we need poetry writers; we don't need discussions, we need a few people hacking it out, typing, getting it down. And we need less snobbery and less poetry gang-factions.

p.s. – the Italians hot for my bod word now. mucho sales on translations over there. Marco Ferreri (spell) has finished directing full length movie, *Tales of Ordinary Madness*, Ben Gazzara acts as Chinaski. They shot some scenes in Venice, Calif. I got drunk with Ferreri and Gazzara, good fellows both.

but this is of the past, it's done, it's the fourth novel now, *Ham On Rye*, page 244. Ought to be finished in a couple of weeks. Then I'm going down to join the San Diego zoo.

• 1982 •

Mike Gold edited Smoke Signals *from New York from 1980 to 1982.*

[To Mike Gold]
[1982]

I'm pretty burned out right now, just off the flu, in from the track, opening the first bottle of wine. Yes, just got new *Smoke Signals*, looks dashing and lively. I'll give it a go, bit by bit. Like to read while crapping, bathing or in bed. Note the bit on d.a. levy. We had a correspondence going, he ran a little book of mine, a long poem, *The Genius of the Crowd*, printed on envelopes as pages. He told me, "They'll read this and still won't understand what you're saying." Those Cleveland cops were squeezing him, for no reason at all. I never met him, but I feel his suicide came too early, maybe not for him but for a few others. His writing was just beginning to evolve. In those days most of the littles were fairly structured and snobbish. When Blazek and d.a. came along with their mimeos it gave a few of us some working room, and I don't know whether we wrote more letters or more poems or more critical articles (ranters really). Sometimes the poems and the letters crossed into one work. It was all right, we played it loose, and it was as exciting a time as I can remember – factory workers and bums playing with the word. I even put out 3 issues of a mag myself.[1] I tried to make my rejects as gentle as possible but some of the responses I got from these were pretty rife and ripe. And shitty. One fairly famous lady poet of that time wrote back after a reject: How can you reject me? What the hell do you know about writing, Bukowski? Where have you been published? You're nothing but a drunk and a lecher!" Well, I was but . . . Then she went on to list her total publications, books and mags and all the places she had read at.

---

1. Bukowski edited and published *Laugh Literary and Man the Humping Guns* for three issues beginning in 1969.

She had no style, cousin, and I felt that her writing showed it.

I could never see how being an oft-published poet could give that person a feeling of being elite. The poets are among the lowest of the breeds – outside their form. And often in it too. For instance, I am a lot more in awe of a plumber than a poet. The plumber can really do me something useful and not get the fat head about it. Also, 9 times out of ten he's a better person to drink with too.

[To Louise Webb]
January 27, 1982

It's been a long time since the old days. Remember the bathtub used up for space for book pages? And cool Jon and excitable Lou, and me sucking on beer.

I hope it's going o.k. for you. I always think of New Orleans and you as one.

I'm drinking about as much as ever but I seem to feel all right most of the time. No feeling in my felt thumb and my liver is probably gone, don't want to think about it. As long as I can sit here and type, that's enough. I am still with Linda Lee and the 3 cats, Butch, Piranna (spell?) and the Manx. The Manx came to the door almost dead one day. We took him in, fattened him up, then a friend came by drunk and ran him over with his car. I saw it. The cat just stared at me as it was happening. We took him to the vet. X-rays. He's not a Manx at all. Vet says somebody cut off his tail. Also he's been shot, pellet still lodged and he was run over, once before – mend of backbone in x-rays He's also cross-eyed. Said he'd probably never walk again. Now he's running, tongue hanging out, cross-eyed. He's a tough crazy.

Is Corrington governor of Louisiana yet? After he went to Hollywood I never heard from him again. Speaking of which, I got drunk with Marco Ferrie (spell?) and Ben Gazzara. Ben is acting in *Tales of Ordinary Madness* directed by Marco. Taken from some of my short stories. But there's something I don't trust about celluloid. I guess it's an old superstition but I get the idea, still, that it kills people. Marco Ferrari, though, seemed a natural and ordinary guy, kind of like a dock worker. He seems to have retained his humanity.

San Pedro is a great little town. The blacks and the whites and the

Mexicans seem to mix all right with very little trouble. at least, I haven't seen any of it like up in L.A.

You seem unhappy with your job. I know it's hell to work for somebody else, it seems senseless and endless. I worked until I was 50, that was eleven years ago. I just decided to let it all go on the writing, I was going to go crazy or suicide the other way anyhow. I got lucky. I wish to hell you could get lucky or maybe feel better.

luck and love,

[To Gerald Locklin]
March 14, 1982

[★ ★ ★] The novel, *Ham on Rye* should be out in the summer, says big John. That means Fall?[1] You ever read about my upbringing you'll know why I've been all these decades trying to straighten the kinks out, and am still working on it. The book begins with the first thing I remember seeing in life and ends around where Pearl Harbor was bombed. (By the way, it looks like Japan is winning the war . . .)

When you consider Fante wrote *Bunker Hill* dictating it to his wife while he was blind and amputated, you've got to know he's circled his field. Went to see him at the hospital recently and he looked pretty bad. He'd just come out of internal hemhorrhaging (I've done that too but can't spell it either). Anyhow, there he was talking about his *next* novel.

I tried to put into his ear that he should write about what had happened to him regarding his own personal and terrible luck but I don't think he will. It would make one hell of a story, you know, how people begin to treat you when you're no longer quite like they are. Well . . . [★ ★ ★]

---

1. Published on July 28, 1982.

[To Gerald Locklin]
May 9, 1982

and I still haven't paid my fucking income taxes, or filed . . . I have this tax accountant in Utah and he phones me drunk on cognac (spell?) and tells me he's working on my case, and how are the horses running?

Hello Lock:

"Lock." "Hey, Lock, ya locked in? haha, ha!"

I can see you now in grammar school listening to that crap; you had no choice but to become a writer. Have you ever noticed that all good writers have strange-sounding names or names that relate, in a sense, to something else?

I sure gotta thank ya for sending *By Land, Sea & Air*.[1] I read your stuff straight through whenever I get it. Sometimes when I'm wading in the dogshit blues and one of your books comes along I get lifted right up and out. Your stuff has this even tenor, it just keeps coming along. Of course, there's always a favorite. With these it came when I was reading "role model." I got that quiet gleeful feeling as I came down to the end of it. Catullus (spell?) couldn't have done any better. a poem like that is something that helps defeat the drag of the centuries.

Glad you used my blurb.

On *Home Planet News* or whatever it's called, I feel that rag's a fake. I think they just like to get submissions and play doll house with them.

Let an old man give you some advice. You know, man, that beer can kill you quicker than anything. You know what it does to the bladder, that amount of liquid just ain't supposed to pass on through the body, not even water. I know it makes for better conversation and keeps you out of alley fights behind the bar (most of the time) but the beer headache and the beer heaves are deathly. Of course, there's nothing like a good old beer shit. But a good wine will add ten years to your life as compared to drinking that green stuff out of the bargain pitchers. I know you prefer the bars and that when you ask for a glass of wine in a bar the tender reaches for this large dusty jug with a splash of dark coagulation hanging to the bottom, which is pure posion. I guess you just gotta go with the beer in the bars. The trouble with bars is that they're just like racetracks: the dullest and the most obnoxious go there. Well, hell, forget it. I'm drinking this

---

1. Published by Maelstrom Press, Long Beach, 1982.

here wine and rambling . . . Just one thing I'd like to ask you? What can a man do about women? When you first meet a woman she seems to show that she is different than the others but then when you get in deep with her she suddenly reverts and becomes *exactly* (with very minor variations) like the one which preceded her and the one which preceded that one and the one that . . .

This letter doesn't call for an answer, chappie, because there ain't none.

[To John Martin]
July 15, 1982

just a note upon the enclosed.

This man thinks a man gets fucked by women because he is "rich and famous." It does bring them around but a man gets fucked because he decides to get fucked. I once thought fucking was a magic and desirable thing. Most often it's just hard work to help the ego.

What makes a man get fucked is his "availability." Long before I became "rich and famous" I just sat round drinking wine and staring at the walls. How I quite made it, I don't know. But I was always around. One night I screwed 3 women in the same night because they were all staying at my hotel room. It's just a matter of being there and feeling like doing it for the hell of it. I wasn't a writer then, I was a drunk. The reason I stopped screwing at one time in my life is because I just didn't think it was worth it. Then I met Linda King and she got me into my old wasted habits again but she was so screwed-up with the sex thing that I had to laugh all upside and bottomside up about it – all the positions, all the tricks, all that crap. I went through it, and I was there and I wasn't there. Then after that busted I decided to do a little research. Which just meant jumping into bed and fucking women because they really want to do it, I think worse than men. So I did my research. And wrote a book.[1]

But this guy here has it all wrong, as most have it that way. Evidently he has problems of where to put his pecker and is envious of one who has

---

1. *Women*, 1978.

put it in many places and at many times. He doesn't know. The poor fuck more than the rich because it's the only recreation they can afford.

It's like one of my women said in the old days, "You may not have much money but you're always around . . ."

The problem with judging another man is that it is always, almost always, done from your perspective. We are not, thank the devil, all alike.

[To Al Fogel]
Augie 6, 1982

[★ ★ ★] Sorry if I'm short or seem short with you sometimes. I have a lot of women troubles no matter which one I'm with. To begin with they don't believe that horseplaying can be a science just as beautiful as setting off an A-bomb or playing a great game of chess. They just want you to tell them how nice their hair looks and to slam that thing into their center. I don't mind doing that, it is just when they become mindless and babble about nothingness. Like Saturday Night Live. Or some god damned movie. "I make my own movies," I tell them. They don't know what the hell I'm talking about.

so you know, even as long as I've been around I come up short and maybe lay some shit on a guy like you who knows that the only fight is the use of the mind and the way against almost impossible odds. I'm sorry and I apologize. It's a deal. I'm sending back your checklist.[1] Send me anything you need signed. To me, a guy like you knows a hell of a lot more about life than the first 5,000 I follow on the freeway to seek whatever action is going. [★ ★ ★]

listen, man, I get pissed. These god damned cunts don't know who I am. Sometimes I think of this guy Roger [*Rodney*] Dangerfield, he's been around, and his humor comes from a driven reality of being and he has some line like, "listen, I demand a little bit of respect around here!" They don't give it to him. What he's really talking about is his damned family, his damned woman, they fuck up his money in large ways, large cars, large stupidities, they don't know the fire he's burning from or the way. But shit, man, they never do. [★ ★ ★]

---

1. Al Fogel, *Charles Bukowski: A Comprehensive Checklist 1946–1982* (Miami, FL: Sole Proprietor Press, 1982).

Ham on Rye is out. now you'll know why I'll bet on anything but the human race.

[To Gerald Locklin]
November 1982

Have been on a drunk and gambling kick, lucky the gambling has paid off quite well but the liver and pancreas are a doormat for the foot of death, along with what's left of the kidneys and lower intestines . . . [★ ★ ★]

I'm honored that you're using *Ham* in one of your classes but only because it's you doing it. But I don't know what you can do with it. Like if you asked me anything about *Ham* the best answer I could give you is, "I don't know." [★ ★ ★]

Give us more women poems. You are the master. And you aren't afraid of them. A most refreshing thing when they've got most of us running because it is a seeming and intelligent thing to do? We must fight back or the world will be almost fag and almost lesbian. All right.

Let me know if you have any new books out and where to buy them. Yow.

[To Gerald Locklin]
December 2, 1982

you still leaning against the '49er? I got enough of the bars about 20 years ago. now I like drinking alone. Hemingway said that was the sign of a true alky. I don't mind being an alky except I get sad for what's left of my liver. but at the age of 62 I figure each day I go on I've beat the odds. I'm drinking now. maybe that's why I'm carrying on like this. like the guy at the bar next to you telling it all. what dull little fellows. they want somebody to talk to. that's one reason I got out of those places: lonely people are boring.

About the women poems, you show much guts and insight there; nobody could write like that unless he lived it.

The problem with the ladies (one of the problems) is that they don't realize we often attack ourselves too. Everybody is afraid of being mentioned as being not too good a person. Hell, there *are* some women who are bitches; there are some blacks, male and otherwise who are unsavory; there are browns like shits and yellows like malaria, and there *are* some Jews who act like Hitler said they did. There is *everything*. Since women's lib everybody is yelling, saying, you can't *say* that, you can't write that about us say the browns, the blacks, greens and the blues . . .

About the *only* one you can write about without rejoinder is the white American male. He won't complain. He won't even care. Which, to me, says one *hell* of a lot for the white American male.

That's us, Jerry, heee, hee, hee . . .

About people who write about other writers they think they once knew, other writers who have gotten lucky or good or both, these types just want a tie-in . . . "I was with Norman Mailer when he got drunk and pissed in his hat . . ." Of course, these types have a right to write anything they want to, their own and only problem being that they can't write too well. I really don't care what they write about *me*: the more vicious and untrue it is the better my books will sell and the further away from the breadline I will be. The worst thing you can do is to respond to these or mention them by name. When a dog barks at you, you don't bark back. Well, sometimes when a *dog* does, I do . . . but you know what I mean. [★ ★ ★]

• 1983 •

[To Gerald Locklin]
January 6, 1983

Thanks for the clippings . . . So we have a play which distorts me and then reviews which further distort, and so it will always be . . . I greet you with a beer after pulling in $525.00 at the track today.

It really doesn't matter what they say as long as I can go on typing, and I keep the people out of here; Linda is by a couple times a week, otherwise all I see are the track faces. I read where Steinbeck was eaten up by visitors; well, if you allow that, you will be eaten. I never liked crowds, even when I was starving.

Note that I'm described as "a very rich writer." I've never heard anybody else described as such, although there are many with more $$$$ than I have. Where these boys get such figures as me making $200,000.00 in one year in Germany, I don't know. Was Mailer ever described as a "very rich writer"? or Bellow? or Michener? People are always pointing things out about me: I'm a drunk or I'm rich or I'm something else. How about the writing? Does it work or doesn't it?

It works for me because it gives me something to do at night and a way to pass the time as time gets down closer to the nub. I guess I sound like a crank but it appears that people more gossip about me than anything else, much of it is word of mouth without factuality. Some women hate me as a "sexist" who have never read but excerpts of my work. Everything gets little bit sick. A woman got off a plane once and told somebody, "Charles Bukowski is dead." It was taken as fact. I got a nice obit in one of the lit mags. Just today I got a letter in the mail from Amsterdam from a lady who says she has heard that I will be there in February. I didn't know this. She goes on to tell me what's best to drink there and so forth . . .

Of course, all this doesn't matter but I can't help noting and it gives me an unclean feeling. Thank god I'm low enough on the totem pole so that the *National Enquirer* doesn't fuck with me.

But all in all, the typing is going all right and that's what I go by: if I can still feel the joy and verve of letting it go then I know they haven't gotten to me. Shapes keep changing but it's still a fight to stay clear of the muck and the swamps and the pits and the traps just like it was in the factories, in the post office. I always liked one thing old Ez said: "Do your work." That's the cure to everything. And you know that, and I know that you're doing your work, just like another old guy Gogol once said, "Laughter through tears."

Note they call me a "beat writer of the 50's." oh my oh my.

All right, we'll just have to out-endure them, as per usual.

[To Gerald Locklin]
January 16, 1983

[* * *] A couple of nights ago Linda King phoned me and told me in a cackling voice that she was going to write a book about our affair and that she was going to use some of my love letters to her. I wished her luck.

People will be that. In a recent article in *Reader* this guy says something like, "Bukowski has now been domesticated by his latest wife and is now happy and so his best writing days are most probably behind him . . ."

Maybe there's *another* Bukowski but this one doesn't have a wife, this one lives alone most of the time. In the same article this guy states that Fante continues to write at his home in Malibu. Fante's in the hospital legless and blind and the Fantes are about to have their home possessed for payment of hospital bills.

I think a lot of this misinformation gets about at gossip sessions. One so-called poet comes up with something and another so-called poet assumes that it's true.

Thanks for sending the review of Fante. I'm sure Joyce will read it to John and it will really give him a high when he needs one. You've certainly done your homework, teach . . .

I agree with you that the earlier work is the best. After that he softened up his work for the *Sat. Ev. Post* and other journals of that ilk. And the movies – well, that's like masturbating day after day and then trying to get it up when the real thing arrives. But Fante was poor, the books weren't selling. Sure, a factory job would have left him with more but he didn't know that. It seemed better to dine at Chasen's and Musso's, meet Faulkner, Sinclair Lewis, so forth . . .

The Catholic thing in Fante's work never bothered me because I was never sure whether he believed or had just been tossed into the Holy ditch. I never asked him. I know when I was a kid the whole Catholic thing seemed very funny to me, rather a circus. It was something to do when there was very little else to do, although those 10 a.m. Sunday masses were *hell*. I got out when I was 12 or 13 and when the priest walked up many years later to give me The Last Rites down at the County Hospital I told him I no longer believed that sort of thing. "Once a Catholic always a Catholic," he told me. "That's not true," I told him and he took a walk. [★ ★ ★]

[To Al Fogel]
February 5, 1983

Thanks for short story and mention of the Buk within. But I hope your old lady really doesn't boil you for reading the Buk. I no longer have an old lady, I've set her free to do her bidding since I think she finds me restrictive. I don't want anybody around who thinks I am putting the lid on them. She was never around anyhow and now that she's not around at all, I'm sure we both feel better.

[★ ★ ★] Just finished a short story tonight called "The Jockey," which I think is one of the best things I've done of late.[1]

You sound a little loose-ended in your last letter. To me you sound like a guy who's been out of the action lately and whose edges are drooping.

I realize that we all need an occasional rest from the gambling war pit. It can finally grind you. Sometimes I've taken a little day or two off and I've accomplished many things. And there's nothing like wasting a couple of days doing nothing. And when you go back into the bloodpit you're really ready.

By the way, I'm onto health foods. Take all the vitamins. Only eat fish or fowl. Fresh produce. Juices. One reason I do this is because I drink

---

1. Collected in *Septuagenarian Stew*, 1990.

heavily and there is my gambling schedule. on top of all this there is my writing disease. Just let me tell you, Al, the worst thing is red meat. This is why many people can't walk, need canes, walkers in their sixties, need to be operated upon for stones and so forth . . . Lay off *salt*. Pepper is not as bad as they say. *sugar* is. Stay away from milk and cream and especially *cheese*.

It's true that most healthfood people are not likeable. They are usually nuts in other ways and are seldom loners or self-contained. I don't like them. But don't let that get you away from the fact that they are right about nutrition. They just make too much of it.

[To Louise Webb]
February 12, 1983

It's always good to hear from you even though I know you are still mad at me for writing a certain short story about you and Jon, but it was too good to resist, and you must understand that I have, still have, the love for both of you, here, now and later.

Maybe it's better you got out of the French Quarter. And if you want it back, it's still there. But like you know, the cities are getting uglier and uglier and the people look, and are the cities. [★ ★ ★]

Your love for Jon was beautiful and holy. I always marveled at it, the almost maddening purity of it, the total, not almost, purity of it. Jon was a very lucky man: you brought him a gift that few men in our time, in our day, ever get.

Please feel as good as you can. You should, you should.

Larry "Ratso" Sloman was editor of National Lampoon *and author of* Reefer Madness *(1979) and* Thin Ice *(1982).*

[To Larry "Ratso" Sloman]
May 7, 1983

Thanks for the book [*Thin Ice*]. I especially liked the conversation of those Hockey Pucks. Although you probably jacked it up a bit. Some of the language is delicious, wish I had writ it, ya.

These poor guy skate, drink, fuck and make money but they know it's going to end and the smartest of them stick a little into the old stocking.

But like they say, at least they got a *taste*, they got out of 8 to 5 and the breadline.

Good book, baby, but I still think I'm prettier than you. Ah well, no matter, we got something else? What is it? I dunno.

Next time you're boning and they're riding top-deck stick your finger up their ass and whistle the star spangled banner, they'll come in a minute.

[To Gerald Locklin]
August 13, 1983

[★ ★ ★] Here are the answers to your questions. I re-enclose your letter so you'll see which answers are to which questions. I'll take them in order.

1. I write a short story a month for *Hi-times*. Started a novel called *Streetwalker*, junked it. Rolling into another called *The Fool*. If it carries itself along I'll finish it; if it becomes rote, or hard work, I'll junk it too.

2. I don't know the $$$ breakdown on fiction vs. poesy, but looking at the reprints of past editions, I'd say it's about equal.

3. Yes, I've gotten letters and phone calls from a large circulation sex-oriented mag I used to write for. I sent them something but they said it was too much, even for them. So I didn't bother any more. Large German mag asked to see something, so I sent them the same story ("The Hog") but they didn't even respond . . . I guess I use this story to get rid of people. I don't like to slant my material. I like a column, a regular outlet somewhere where I can bust loose. Everything else is too tight, too stupid.

4. *Barfly* sits, as bar flies do. It might work into something some day. It's not a bad film script, it's just that many people with money think a barfly is not worth putting up on the screen. Of course, the producers are wrong, but they usually are . . . On *Tales of Ordinary Madness*, I didn't recognize the poet as anybody I ever knew. He was such a friendly fellow, smooth mug, and he never got so drunk he fell through a window or anything like that. His insanity was drab. It was just an Italian idea of an American poet, and they owe me money. That's probably another Italian idea, that I don't need money. What's a poet?

5. It feels good to write all of it. Once you sit down in front of the typer it's like you're watching a movie, a good one. Sorry, but it's all the same: poem, story, novel, I'm happiest at finishing interviews so I can get back to the writing, the bottles the racetrack.

6. Yes, I drink when I write fiction. Why not? I like things to be entertaining. If *I* feel entertained at this machine maybe somebody else will feel that way too . . . The typewriter is the only way; it seems to make it official as it splatters out of the brain. Sound, action . . . music on the radio . . . picking up the wine glass . . . smoking . . . What a love affair! Never any arguments here.

7. Summer 1984? If I'm alive it will still be the same: the poem the story, the novel. If there has been a change, let's say it's this: I'm inventing more, taking less from my actual life. I get tired of myself and I'm sure others must too . . . Of course, I think more of death but nothing comes through. It's a burnout. I'm ready to die, it's nothing. But you know, typing feels so good, and sitting in my shorts drinking at night, looking out the window. It's fine . . .

8. People like to ask me, "Did that really happen to you?" And I used to tell them. Now, I don't. I think it's good for them to wonder. O.k., then, *most* did and what *didn't* should have.

9. No. I haven't been sued, mostly, I think, because I haven't exaggerated upon the actuality of things. I know that this sometimes isn't enough, but I think most people are glad that I put them into my works, even the rattlesnake people, like even a bad mention is better than not being noticed, what? I know that some things have been written about me and, the more gross and untrue they are, the better I like them. It's funny.

10. The critics in print are pretty fair. I get bad-mouthed by people who have never read my work, and by some who have but have read things into it. I am supposed to have an evil tinge (tindge?) about me,

strangle babies in their cribs, walk about in underwear a month gone unwashed and so forth and so forth. Some of my stories are about lunatic and criminal people, therefore I am lunatic and criminal like that. The most ridiculous charge is that I'm a sexist pig. If one will read the body of my work, they will see that where ridicule or attack falls, the male receives just as much as the female. There are shitty women just as there are shitty men; the fact being, that I have lived with women, and some of them have been worse than shitty. I reserve the right to state that fact if I find that it fits into the flow of some work I am into. In American society about the only one you can safely attack is the white male, preferably if he's a Nazi. And I don't want to sit around doing that night and day.

11. Oh, I see I overlooked a bit. No, no more readings. I never liked to read but I feel that when they got their money up I gave them something to remember. On promotional tours I got sucked into *one* of those, never again. One morning in Paris they shook me out of bed, beastly hungover, got me into the patio at 9:30 a.m. and interviewed me. Before the day was over I had given 6 interviews. There's just not that much to say. It's all in the writing. But people need that. They need to poke. They can poke you to pieces.

12. The recent Bukowski "exposés" in little mimeo editions of 500 are sad.[1] People who have met me at one time or the other and think it's a big thing. But again, it's curious when I hear what they were thinking at the time, things like: Bukowski was afraid I would steal his woman. Bukowski was afraid some young writer would take his place. Many other things like that, which I never thought of at all. It's only that *they* would have thought that way if they had been Bukowski, and that's why they weren't Bukowski.

13. Christ, that's enough. one thing: I'm glad *you're* interested.

---

1. Perhaps referring to David Barker, *Charles Bukowski Spit in My Face* (Salem, OR: D. Barker, 1982) or Jory Sherman, *Bukowski: Friendship, Fame & Bestial Myth* (Augusta, GA: Blue Horse Publications, 1981).

[To John Martin]
October 11, 1983

[★ ★ ★] Linda appears to be getting worse. I don't know if I'll ever be able to write that novel. People who think I have it made and that I live in peace and glory, they just don't know. I've lived with so many insane women. I believe that Women's Lib has contributed greatly toward pushing some of them over the line. It makes them so concerned and conscious of their own identities and needs that they fail to consider the feelings of the men they live with. I'm certain that not all women are this way but many who are on the edge of hysteria because of aging, because of failure in what they individually wanted to do, to be . . . that the easiest out for them is to take extreme umbrage and revenge against the man or men they are living with. This eases their consciousnesses [?*consciences*] and gives them the needed scapegoat, the needed excuse for their diminished lives. And if a man fights back against their in-fed railings, then he is a male chauv pig. And if he doesn't, he becomes a podosperm and/or a spiritual eunuch. The streets and the universities are full of them. The ladies have their balls in a bag, and the women are beginning to look and dress and act like men and the men are doing themselves in to appear to be all things ladylike. What it comes to is that each man must save himself, even if it means living alone, which, with conditions as they are, doesn't seem at all a difficult thing to do. I am still beset by erections but after the battalions of harpies I've lived with I really fear to engage said stiffness upon new females because of the terrible price attached. As I get older, if I get older drinking away my sorrows, I'll most probably need a nurse more than the other, and then will still probably still get sucked off upon the stairway or trapped and strapped in my wheelchair. Ah well, or not so well, we can't change the workings, we can only attempt to avoid them as long as possible. And John, I know you will never use this paragraph as a New Year's greeting but you are forgiven.

Listening to Bruckner, and it's a beautiful and magic night anyhow,

---

[To Larry "Ratso" Sloman]
November 11, 1983

[★ ★ ★] Jesus, I'm hobnobbing with the jockeys' agents and horse trainers now. Got drunk with some of them the other night. I now got Turf Club parking and owners and trainers stickers all over my car. I park right up front free and have passes to turf club and box seats at Santa Anita and Los Alamitos. I play the day meet at Anita and then drive over the bridges and play the night races. Fuck writing.

I'm a better horseplayer than all of them. They tried to get my system out of me while I was drunk but I layed them some fake leads. Let 'em find their own way home . . .

Got my photo taken in the winner's circle at Anita, in color, man, it's hanging on my wall. Big thrill. Pincay up. I bet the horse that finished 2nd. [★ ★ ★]

• 1984 •

[To John Martin]
Early February, 1984

[★ ★ ★] There's no New York publisher who can buy me away from Black Sparrow. Let alone these jack-offs with their mimeo machine souls. You do decades of work to publish me in fine format that has allowed my work to go world-wide and they think I'm just going to say, "All right, go ahead, what do you want?" Where were they when I was in the Post Office? Where were they when things were so impossibly and maddeningly awful? You were there. With help. Now they think I'm just going to offer over a bit of work, like that.

They make me sick. It's an insult to me and to you. [★ ★ ★]

[To Suzy? ————]
March 1, 1984

Hello Suzy:

Yes, there are many people out there who dislike my work, but for me, it's the same: if I met these in person I would probably dislike them too, so we're even. On the matter of women, many women are bitches and killers and I've slept with a few of them. If a black or an oriental or a midget is a son of a bitch I will say so. People are offended because they are offensive. About the only person you can write badly of in literature and not hear about it is the *white american male*. Which must tell you something . . .

In this country, the male is dominated by the female, they went completely under to the Woman's Lib movement, so much so that most of them almost look like and act like women. About the only difference between them is that the female has breasts and her ass is bigger. Sexual parts different, yes, but I think some of those guys stick their dicks up their asses hoping to have pussies. And the worst male(?) is the one who is worried about Female Rights. This is nothing but open beggary, trying to score points in the most demeaning fashion.

I don't look at the female as inferior to me, only different than I and there will always be problems because of this difference, along with the joys. The best thing any person can do is to be as much the way as he (she) wants to be rather than being moulded by mass dictate, style, so forth. Of course, most people are completely wiped out by the educational system, church, country and the need to survive. And they will be offended by anything that goes against what they have been stuffed with, and they are *stuffed, stuffed turkeys, stuffed sausages, stuffed bags of shit*. Even death doesn't do them honor because it just takes meat, not soul, not true gut, not anything interesting at all. I say some of this here because I get weary of my work being attacked by moths . . . Christ, I'm almost forgetting to laugh at them . . . ow . . .

The movie *Tales of Ordinary Madness* was ridiculously bad. Gazzara looked like a satisfied dullard. Oh boy, holding to that girl's legs down by the sea and moaning out one of my early poems about the atom bomb . . . But almost all of it was worse than bad. And Gazzara always hitting on the wine bottle but never getting drunk. Water, what? I sat through that movie drinking bottles of wine and screaming against the whole atrocity. I wasn't mad but what a *disgust* I felt.

Luck with your novel. I dislike rules, they are made to be broken. But I'd say the best thing to go by is – never write unless you really *feel* like writing, it has to come out like hot turds the morning after a good beer drunk. So, listen, I'm going . . . going to crack open a new bottle of vino and play with this machine, I hope to die upon this motherfucker . . . o.k.

[To Al Berlinsky]
March 15, 1984

No, Hank Malone is wrong, I'm not dead as per report of his friend just back from the West Coast. Every four or five years somebody announces that I'm dead. Why they have the need to do this, I'm not sure. It's usually done by other writers and writers are a fairly ill breed. Then too, I live as isolated as possible because I feel better that way, and if

I don't answer a letter or the phone, then I'm dead, you see. Some day they'll be right and it will be one of the few times they were ever right about anything. Don't consider me bitter, just accurate. [★ ★ ★]

Have been reading *The Passionate Years* by Caresse Crosby. All these people did was travel about, eat and party, and knock upon the doors of the famous. They also abused the peasants without realizing it. Caresse published one of my first stories and I always wondered why. Now I know. It was about a man with delicate hands sitting in a jail. Shit. [★ ★ ★][1]

Douglas Goodwin is a Los Angeles poet, author of Slamming It Down *(Santa Monica: Earth Rose Press, 1993).*

[To Douglas Goodwin]
March 15, 1984

I don't know why they sometimes compare me to Henry Miller. I always had trouble reading him. He'd go on all right a while and then he'd get astral or fluffily literary and I'd get discouraged. Comparison will happen and I suppose it's better to be compared than ignored.

On Hemingway, I suppose it's the simple line but the man had no humor. As simple lines went, I preferred Saroyan's to Hemingway's. The early Saroyan, I mean. But Saroyan was too sweet, too optimistic; it worked well in his stories of the depression but when things got better it really sounded out of key. Then he changed too, for the worse. The paragraphs fattened and it made hard reading.

You're right on Fante and Céline and James M. Cain, each had something that helped me. There was also a Russian, Turgenev, who wasn't bad. And Sherwood Anderson, he exulted and exalted in the short and simple line, maybe a little too much so.

As for the attackers, I have been accused of "slipping" ever since my first chapbook came out when I was 40 years old. Many of the professors don't like it that I don't consort with them, and they don't like where I came from. It bothers them. For centuries these literary slickers have been

---

1. At the end of this letter Bukowski types out his poem "The Lost Generation," published in *You Get So Alone at Times That It Just Makes Sense* (1986).

fooling the people and they just pass the palm on down. They don't want anything to upset their doll's house. The best way a fake can cover is to call somebody else a fake. Their attacks on me are an affirmation that I'm doing things right. I just go on with what I'm doing. [★ ★ ★]

Gerald Locklin's 1984 books were The Phantom of the Johnny Carson Show *(Los Angeles: Illuminati),* The Case of the Missing Blue Volkswagen *(Long Beach, CA: Applezaba Press), and* Fear and Paternity in the Pauma Valley *(Detroit, MI: Planet Detroit).*

[To Gerald Locklin]
June 22, 1984

[★ ★ ★] Well, there are women and there are women. Mostly women. Some will reach under a table and squeeze a stranger's balls when you go to the bathroom to piss, then if you catch wind of the act they'll accuse you of "jealousy." But *reverse* the act on them, they can't handle it, not at all. Shit, I don't *mean* grab a guy's balls! You know what I mean . . .

Hey, I've submitted to you a proposed foreword. 2 copies. If it works for you, please send on to your man. If it doesn't work, then I'm glad the Celtics did it to your boys.

Sucking on the wine. Should work out with a few poems now. Habit, you know.

Thanks for all the books! Some I haven't seen. Have had some great reading.

you big fucking bear of grace, keep going . . .

p.s. – When I speak of "undiscovered talents," I mean a vaster fame, if not a la Mailer, maybe S. Bellow or who the hell have you . . .

[*Enclosure:*]

> June 22, 1984
> Gerald Locklin is one of the great undiscovered
> talents of our time. For decades now, I have enjoyed
> his work. Whenever one of his little chapbooks have
> come out or I have gotten hold of a magazine with
> some of his work in it, that day, especially, has been a
> good one for me. I say "day" because I read his work

right off, prose or poetry, a couple of pages or many pages. I have never been let down. I have been picked up, lifted up, tossed into that rare area: excellent writing, writing with verve, writing that laughs, writing that reads easy yet says something. That's a good package.

Locklin often attacks himself, or anything or anybody else that needs it, but always with grace and sometimes with wonderment and most always with a humor that I can only describe as most admirable considering the conditions he writes about. He is quite good at writing about the man–woman relationship, or, if you will, non-relationship. His ear for dialogue between the male and the female have [*sic*] not been so well done since, I'd say, the days of James Thurber. And with Locklin there is no side-taking, no preaching. He just tunes us in and lets us have it the way it is. And that takes courage no matter how easy he makes the writing seem to us.

He can write about sitting at a bar and drinking beer or shooting a game of pool, or he can talk about basketball, and it all fits together, it's all there: defeat and victory, fixations and traps, the daily going-on until it ends for us.

It has been my pleasure to speak very well of this man and now I think it will be your pleasure to read him. Fine then. Proceed.

Charles Bukowski

[To William Packard]
July 13, 1984

I like your sample rejects. They're funny but, lo, the recipients wouldn't laugh. I was a magazine editor twice (little mags) but happily for only a short period. But during those stretches I learned how precious and nasty and self-assured these poesy-dispensers can be. And the worse they wrote, the viler they were. I made the mistake, in the beginning, of sending out personal two or three page rejects explaining what didn't work for me, what I thought writing could and should be (with some luck). I remember one night writing a 5 page reject.

One lady sent me (in return) many pages of burning pink reply in which she listed all the magazines she had been published in and the names of the editors, plus all the places she had read her poetry (with dates) and she also told me she was in *The Blue Book*. She also called me a drunk and a letch. – Now you know that anybody who calls anybody a "letch" is fundamentally fucked in the backwoods of their mind. She also asked me, "Where have *you* been published, Mr. Bukowski? It seems to me that . . ." blah blah blah . . . Being married at the time and not feeling too good about it, I opened a pint and answered this lady with a 6-pager. She did not respond. Again.

There seems to be a lot of snobbery with people who write, even those who write well. What I consider special is a good plumber or auto mechanic, or a jock who can come through on the rail to get it at the wire when I have a few bob riding.

So, when you reject yours, it's always going to be a problem, they are going to believe it's for a wrong reason. There is hardly such a thing as a modest writer. Especially a modest bad writer. But if you only have to deal with them through the mails it's not so bad. It's the personal visits that are repelling: since you write, since they write, bingo, and therefore they expect something like a brotherhood or a sisterhood. I prefer cats as companions. I see enough people every day and the best thing about most of those is that they don't write.

Anyhow, a sample reject enclosed.

[*Enclosure:*]

> This is a rejection slip, and most of what we receive must be rejected otherwise our magazine would be ten miles long and nobody could afford to buy it even if we could afford to print it.
>
> We too have been rejected and will be rejected again and again. In this business you must expect it. And when it happens you can either quit or write better or try another magazine.
>
> It's true that sometimes a rejection is unwarranted. Our opinion is neither final or anything else. It's only

our taste or lack of it. But we can only proceed as best as we think we might know how.

It's good that you did try us and allow us to read your work(s). From what arrives in the mail is where we must go. Without submissions we would be hapless and helpless. This rejection does not mean that we will not look at further of your submissions if you so desire to try us again. So this rejection is personal and yet not so personal, and if you do try us again and we find we must, once again, reject you, perhaps at least by then we will have a new rejection form to send you so you won't become too bored and unhappy with us, or perhaps there will, at last, be no need for a rejection, which will please you, which will please us and which, we hope, will please our readers. Otherwise –

Stephen Kessler was editor and publisher of Alcatraz, *and a book reviewer for the* Los Angeles Times.

[To Stephen Kessler]
September 10, 1984

Sure, run *Traffic* as a broadside in some future, if it suits you.

This poem has had some butt kicking and some traveling . . . First accepted by *New York Quarterly*, which then folded and now has returned.

The "Mailbox" broadside is all right, I guess, but when I read it in broadside form I felt it a bit cruel. The writer talking down the not-so-lucky ones. But my nerves jumped and I was goaded into writing it. No excuse, I know. But I'm not an editor or a publisher and my mailbox gets heavy with "works" of art. I drown in paper here. Plus the letters. Mostly from young girls who think I might be interested. Young girls develop into large problems. Nothing's free. Once in a long while I do get a good work and I try to suggest a place to submit it, and I've been happy to see some of this get into print. I don't think I've made any great discoveries, except maybe John Fante, and H. L. Mencken found him first almost 50 years ago. [★ ★ ★]

[To Al Fogel]
September 27, 1984

[* * *] Well, maybe you need woman trouble to keep you stirred. I used to feed on that. But women don't understand the gambler, and if you write on the side there's a battle for time with them. You know, sitting in a movie is one of the biggest wastes for me. I like to create my own action. Watching those monkeys on celluloid getting all fucked-up over commonplace nonsense, well, it de-balls me. I like the popcorn and the large Dr. Pepper, though. But it's no match to that bottle of wine next to the typer when it's running hot: 6F:I:07 4/5.

The track, at times, is a big zero too. When you're scoring heavy, there's a certain sense of rhythm, a music, you step light, you glide, and it carries over into other areas of your life. Winning is not detrimental. We're only here for one whirl. But when you run into a losing day or a couple of them, you're back in the factory again, it slugs you, drains . . . There will always be trouble enough . . . No need to tear up money and substance. Anybody can be a professional loser, most are. So, I work to alter that. The car runs better then, the sun shines better and that m.f. death doesn't get as big a bite. Yeah. Still, it's *War All the Time*.

[To John Martin]
November 22?, 1984

Well, I read *War All the Time* and I think the poems hold up the pages. You made a good selection, placement and balance of poems against each other. As they run off, it's almost like a story form. You know what you're doing. It takes instinct and time to make such an arrangement. Even though it's work, you like what you're doing. That's one reason why Black Sparrow Press continues both as a business and a pleasure.

I'm sure there are many others who have thought that since you did it, they could too. No way. You could even tell them what to do, they could still use the same writers and they would fail. They all want it the easy way. They want to sit on couches and chatter and roll joints. They pose, they don't do.

It's the luck of my life that both you and Carl Weissner took an interest in my work and at a time when there wasn't much. Carl too works like a fury. You might as well: if you're going to do something you might as well do it. And you've both done it. [★ ★ ★]

[To Stephen Kessler]
December 28, 1984

Thanks for sending review of *War* from your column. Your words are kind and, let's hope, accurate. The Bukowski-haters are still out there and for this I am grateful. When these stop gnawing at their syzygies I will know that I'm finished.

I write the BMW poems to piss off those who hated me when I lounged upon the park benches. If I get my American Express Gold Card you can damn well bet I'll write a bit more to spoil their sated evenings. I like to play. Not that I write for them, more – from them. Then other times I forget them entirely, which is more than they can do with me.

Actually the poems 1981–84 are only about one-sixth of the output. I'm not saying that the 5/6th left out are all very good but there's a chance that a few are. John Martin has quite a buildup of unpublished material from a couple of decades. There's a very good chance, if the world is still here, that John Martin can publish a new Bukowski book each year for a good 5 or 6 or 7 years, maybe longer depending upon how long I continue to drink this good wine. Of course, that will all be beyond me: I'll be down in Hades playing the Horses.

Overseas fame while having limited fame here is the best, the gods are looking after me: I can walk through a dozen supermarkets or up and down the main drags of major cities (American) and nobody will bother me. This allows me to live a normal life which only I can despoil. Most indents upon me are made through the mail. An occasional rare and real letter deserves an answer. But to the young ladies who want to crawl under the sheets with me – I shrug off to the next. Sex is nice and serves the libido (or however you spell it) but all the rest spells overprice for value given. Fuck it. Not.

And there's always agony enough to keep comfort from setting in. I wish there weren't. I don't want to feel bad to write good. I really write better when I feel good. I am not afraid of happiness. But the deck keeps coming up with bad cards. Well? [★ ★ ★]

• 1985 •

[To Stephen Kessler]
January 15, 1985

[★ ★ ★] Got your letter. Yes, I know you are an Ace. And can handle such matters such as interviews much better than almost anybody. But I've got to say "no" because I'm just burned-out over such things. Went through an experience – twice – of talking my ass off for hours to people who were going to do a biography on me. Nothing happened. Not that that is important, it's just the energy of the hours wasted. Then did a film bit with some Italians and one other guy and they all got to squabbling, stealing from one another, threatening lawsuits, all that . . . the cans just sit there full of hours of my babble . . . Finally did another film bit for another group and it worked, was shown full blast . . . Then talked *for sixty hours* for a video. I believe it began showing on National TV in France, prime time, this Jan. 7 or 8. It is supposed to run in segments of from 3 to 6 minutes for a great many nights, depending on how long it takes somebody to bomb the station.

What I'm trying to say here is that *I'm sick of talking about myself.*

I need some relief from that. 8 or 9 times a month I turn down interviews and readings. Some of these interviews are from European newspapers. Or mags. Supposed to coincide with the bringing out of a new book in translation. I have to tell everybody the same thing – I can't do it for a while. It just has to rain some more to fill the dam.

The main thing about writing is to write, not to talk about writing.

I remember, maybe a couple of decades ago, every time I opened a mag it seemed as if there were an interview with Henry Miller, A. Ginsberg or Burroughs. Miller sometimes said something but G. just ranted on in hot air and Burroughs was bored and boring. But they didn't know how to say "no" and so here they continued to appear here and there, just saying *anything*. [★ ★ ★]

[To William Packard]
February ?, 1985

Got the *new NYQ*, the bird has arisen! Long may it flay and fly and fuck and fling and feast! [★ ★ ★]

What I liked best was the James Dickey excerpt (on and almost done with 2nd bottle, forgive typos . . . typoes . . . potatoes . . .) about writer's blocks . . . What he says is very true: not enough time to do it. What he means is not that he is torn away by the Superbowl Game or waxing his horse, what he means is doing all the damnable things we are forced to do or the fuckers will come get us: paying the bills, singing to the IRS and Franchise, keeping tires properly inflated, getting birthday and Xmas presents, seeking Christ or the Devil, getting your license plate tabs, teeth cleaned, new shoes, intestine check, arguments with the opposite sex; 90,000 empty faces at a sporting event; death, sickness, why go on?

I once wrote a short story about a man who decided to do nothing about all these things, and it ends up with him crawling under his bed (alone) and pissing into his hanky as they gassed him and came in with their guns to kill him . . . The editors said it was "unrealistic" so I tore it up.

A month later a black woman, one B. Love, was shot to death over a matter of an unpaid gas bill.

Then there are always some people who need us for one reason or another. Sometimes the reasons are right or other times the other. But it's hell to be a final judge.

o.k., let's say we swept verily everything out and concentrated on *writing*. What would we be then? Proust in a corklined room? Nicely insufficient. If we are to put the word down well we are going to have to realize the rights of rats, roaches, bores and Parking Meter girls. If we don't get the whole flex we are fucked right up the twisted typer ribbon. I am not saying we must do the proper and taught thing but we should do the instinctive thing.

The human and the word can't be separated. Do anything else and the lie will come through. It's just one of those god damned laws. And a good one.

James Dickey always bothered me because he seemed to be writing from a position of comfort. I am prejudiced toward those who rise from the gutter. But being *down* doesn't necessarily preclude goodness either. It is possible to come from any area and still produce a substantial and entertaining art. Like some, no, one of your writers talks about writing upon yellow lined paper in the morning. Although I am usually puking my guts out about this time, yellow lined paper belongs too, according to the lightning it brings . . . Let us be friends together, but not gather. The lice roam the dome of Buddha. See us helpless now, pretending.

[To John Martin]

4-late day-night, 1985

For me, the same taste is still there when I sit down to the machine as there was when I was in the factories or the post office or starving it out trying to be a writer. If anything the words now seem to arrive with more luck and order, less waste. It comes from doing and doing, I suppose.

I can't see getting older as anything but a benefit in this arena. Death gets closer but even that seems a good thing – I've always enjoyed the ends of parties better than the beginnings.

The knockers have always been there, first because I came from the streets and later because I escaped them. Also, I have never consorted with the practitioners and I believe that this has pissed them. For me, I always thought writing meant to write.

Others become angry and edgy because they think I live a happy and contented life. They think that things have become too good for me, therefore, they formulate, I can no longer type.

Actually, they know very little of what is occurring in my life, and hoping for signs of decay, they invent them. Poor darlings, if only they could put their energies to a more generous use. No wonder there is so much room for me.

[To John Martin]

May ?, 1985

[* * *] All kinds of crap tumbling down here. I have at my fingertips one of the wildest novels a man could ever write. If you think the Father-scene was a mad laughing howler, you just don't know. This has 40,000 layers. But I believe in kindness toward those who really need it, it's far more important than any literary exposition.

Also, the lack of royalties of any kind is what a writer must expect. I remember once reading a Sherwood Anderson book he wrote about his life: "There I was being taught at all these universities and I had to borrow money to keep going."

All this reminds me of years ago when 2001 pulled in its horns and Carl and Montfort passed the message on to me, "The Bukowski boom is over."[1] Now, once again, there seems this withdrawal of support, and that's all right except I feel connotations of cowardice in other men I'd rather not see.

At the same time, I have this odd feeling that my writing is getting better and better, that each word placed seems to fit exactly where it belongs in humor, grace and with some fine luck.

I know that you are having your troubles too and plenty of them. This is the way it goes. You can't fool me – often times after busting your ass all day long in the office you want to come in for a breather and you find walls of yowling over nothing when all you want to do is inhale and exhale, just a moment. One thing you've got going: Barbara really helps Black Sparrow fly with her book design work.

Anyhow, Dillinger would laugh at both of us, especially me.

[To William Packard]

June 13, 1985

Just got *NYQ* #27, Jesus Christ, you gave me a spread! This has to be my finest honor, photos, craft interview, poems *and* there I am spread throughout your editorial. Like I said, it took some guts on your part, glad you've got them, but you're going to hear some croaking from those tender frogs upon their lily pads.

What I liked best in #27, though, was the editorial. You took the whole game apart and held it before them, saying, this is what you are and it's hardly very much. Your phone is going to be ringing and your mail is going to be singeing with that indignant and hysterical hatred that only the truly guilty are capable of.

---

1. "2001" is the German publishing company Zweitausendeins (Frankfurt), which published four Bukowski titles between 1974 and 1980.

I've got to mark you down as the first man, in your position, to move things around more than a bit. Old Ez woulda been proud, and it's well you used him too, a la editorial. [★ ★ ★]

p.s.s. – and today rec. your acceptance slips for the *five* poems. This is about all the good luck I can handle. They better not drop the Bomb for a little while yet . . .

[To William Packard]
June 25, 1985

Much strife on the home front, and so I escaped the screaming by going to the night quarterhorse track over the bridge, pulled in $150, came back, and I suppose to console myself further, I opened *NYQ* #27, re-read the craft interview, holding Whitman in the palm of my left hand, I found:

". . . first thing I remembered writing was about a German aviator with a steel hand who shot hundreds of Americans out of the sky during World War *II* . . ."

Ow! one with Céline!

I feel that it's safe to say you've caught plenty a dung for running this interview, especially from the prim, the soft and the entrenched. Now they'll say you're hiding a Nazi under your rug.

Sorry, Wm Packard, I must have typed it up wrong – I meant world war *one*: (1914–1918). see Wilfred Owen and so forth . . .

You see, when I wrote my aviator-with-the-steel-hand bit, I was about 13, say in 1933, laying in bed with the worst case of Acne Vulgaris on record, or so the medics gleefully informed me. Adolph was around but he was still just moving his pawns on the chess board. Shooting those Americans out of the sky was my childish revenge for the boils which festered me, along with a brutal father and an indifferent mother. Rebellion is often caused more by reaction than by reason. I think I explain this all fairly well in my novel, *Ham on Rye*.

It appears that I've always been the victim of rumors:

"He beats his women . . ."

"He doesn't pay child support . . ."

"He's a child-molestor . . ."

"He died, just the other day . . ."

A couple of years back I happened to be reading an interview of a local poet in one of the papers and the poet asked his English prof, "What do you think of Bukowski?" And the prof answered him, "He's a fucking Nazi. He'd sell his mother out for a nickel."

I don't know *what* causes all this crap but some of it must simply be envy, and that's worse than sad. I only wish my fellow scribblers had just a bit more class.

Anyhow, it was World War *one*. And if I were a Nazi I would be the first one to come out and say so.

I hope you haven't caught too many outrageous arrows.

[To John Martin]
June?, 1985

You've made a living at it, and mostly have published what you've wanted to, perhaps not so much at the beginning when you tended to listen more to "literary" voices who wanted to point you toward "prestige," but more and more you've become the gambler, one who gambles but still tends to win – out of style and knowledge, instinct. What sells is not necessarily good and what doesn't sell can really be bad, rather than a misunderstood Art-form. There are all manners of this admixture. Running a good show takes an Eye which can separate the bull from the bullshit. You do your work with an energy which boggles the slack, lackadaisical wishes and dreams of those who think things might arrive without the good fight.

They talk you down for making things work when they can't make things work; their envy is wrought out of their pitiful weakness. You simply go ahead, continue, while they rail at their seeming misfortune which is only brought about by a gross laziness and a licorice stick-like backbone.

You are the publisher, the editor, the script reader, the bill-collector, the publicist, and Christ knows what else, while you listen to the so-called Great Ones moaning and groaning over the telephone about all manners of trivial animosities, the tender two-bit troubles that trouble every living creature but which *they* feel particularly set-upon because of their very sensitive and chosen, so-called, God-given tenfold genius.

You do your fucking work and you do it well, very well, but what bothers me, even if it doesn't bother you, is what I consider your almost lack of recognition for what you do, have done, continue to do, relentlessly and with force. I dare say you've published a body of literature for almost three decades that stands unsurpassed in the history of publishing in America. Yet, what is said about you? Not that you need it, only that I need it for you. I prefer Champions not to go unnoticed.

Your problem is that in doing your work you have forsaken the time to go to all the cocktail parties and to kiss the asses of the media and university creatures who would boost you into the circle of their dull and death-like prominence.

Don't worry, the Bomb will be soon enough and if not, the record of your accomplishments will be there, Black Sparrow, you foolish wonderful kind son of a bitch.

[To William Packard]
July 3, 1985

glad the typo didn't bring on a bevy of Nazi hunters, I was getting ready to pack it away with Céline and Ezra, and Knut Hamsun. You're right, the reader doesn't read that closely – unless they really hate you and are looking for something and everything. I once wrote something about e. e. Cummings and in print it came out "e. Cummings." This bit elicited a two page ranting attack on me: "Everybody else calls him e. e. Cummings but Bukowski, no, he calls him 'e. Cummings'! Who the hell is Bukowski?" . . . Two pages of this stuff, asserting that this was the key to the weakness in my character. Of course, it was a printer's error. And I didn't respond to the attack, figuring anybody that dumb was best left to slide on away. Even met the fellow at a house one night where I was drinking. He sat in a blither of hatred but I still didn't tell him that the whole matter was a typo. Didn't matter that much to me and the fellow has long since vanished.

Hot as Hades here tonight, woman with back and mind-problems, cat with broken leg, and I myself feel fitful, star-crossed, near useless. But . . . *here's the bottle!* Such a good companion, tonight I start with this bottle of cabarnet sauvignon . . . Soon the earth will seem to be not such a bad place. ah, give a man a bottle and give a man some walls! [★ ★ ★]

[To William Packard]
July 15, 1985

You gave intros to the poets in the 1950's at the readings at YMHA Poetry Center? Jesus, William, how old are you? Not that I have anything against *age* – the longer a man lives and still keeps his senses, the more amazing it is. Just somehow, in my mind, I had you around 38. Dumb of me, I know. Here you mention those now gone: Eliot, Frost, Capote, e. e. Cummings . . . Cummings could really cut the ice. What a fucker, he laid the lines down like slabs of sizzling bacon.

Well, I'm still here, though went to see my Chinese doctor today – easy on the drinks and smokes. Asked me if I could still get it up, told him: no problem. Also, met my old doc at the track Sunday – my body used to stiffen like a rock of pain while I worked the Post Office and I got dizzy spells, so he used to write me my little excuse notes for the P.O. He always let me sit in his office and drink beer while I waited my turn, he'd stalk in and say, "Shit, that woman has cancer of the ass, her whole ass is eaten away and she won't die!"

Anyway, he was drunk at the track, as per his custom, and I went up to him and said, "Looky, here, Doc, I want some free medical advice . . ." and I showed him arm and asked, "Is this skin cancer?" And he looked, said, "You gotta get that cut off." And I told him, "I just wanted to know what it is, not what to do . . ."

"The other day I only had 7 patients," he told me, "and the following day I only had one. You come to see me, I'm a cheap doctor."

"How do you select your horses?" I asked.

"The bartender selects them for me," he responded.

I knew then that I had to get away from him but he kept talking, then they were at the gate.

"Pardon me," I said, "but I have to watch them run."

He hollered after me as I walked away, "Why the fuck do you have to watch them run? It won't make any difference."

He was right, of course. [★ ★ ★]

[To William Packard]
mid-July, 1985

Is it me or is it them? I've met backyards and blooming top-floor ladies blossoming against the sun, I've been hacked and deterred and made more than glum by their ripping complaints, usually in the early morn as if, night-stored and energized, they are released upon me at the opening of a new day.

Is this what we live for and with?

And – even altering all considerations – considering ourselves guilty and at blame – would we even get to the point of this constant harangue, endless, dementing, vengeful?

Sex, love, duty, God, family are not to be bargained with against happiness, and we don't even ask happiness, just a little less pain.

Sometimes after listening to days, years of the female screaming face I wonder if I am really guilty of the cause of these dark, morbid and ever-continuing circus acts. This might be an unkind description of the act – but, if I have a weakness, it's kindness. And, that traps me in. No matter what the female rails.

I've met them of all sizes, stations, educations and experiences and their most central energy has seemed to be a constant anger against anything around – the slightest hinderance against their wants bringing forth all manner of cursing and vindictiveness.

So, it's not only me, it's everybody and everything, and Christ knows, I am discouraged enough by general and ungeneral happenings.

but *where* does this constant fidgetry come from, galling against any chance of a decent day?

PMS, indeed, PMS forever.

Men, too, have problems, most of them which they head right on into without the flap of aplomb and excuse of gender and championship or the lack of it, they hold up the corner bank or just drink themselves quietly to death. Or whatever they have to do to get done what must be done. And when they are smashed in the loss of their gamble, they know that that is the workings and that is it. That's not macho, that's simply guts.

Anyhow, hell, it's been a long night around here and so I type this manner of things. Lucky, for all of us, male and female, there are other things about, other sights, other scenes, something to get us away from all this, and when death comes it will hardly be a task – not unless they follow us, programmed into their unhappiness.

[To William Packard]
near august ending, 1985

Glad your book[1] finally found a printer, it's amazing that in our age such a censorship exists. Yet I've known other cases where the printer has refused on basis of content. Most printers I've met are smug dolts and also fairly unlived. Censorship exists due to the fact that our educational institutions don't educate and the Church is still around dragging its feet one thousand years behind the times. False morality is the disease of a people who are told what to think and how to act from an early beginning; few ever use their own thought processes to question what they are taught. Talk about the living dead, they crawl like flies upon this turd of an earth.

About getting married, if this destroys me as a writer then I deserve to be destroyed.[2] Christ knows, some of those shack jobs tried hard enough to put my balls into their purses. Also, drinking was long ago supposed to have destroyed me. I have been drinking heavily for 50 years and I feel fine. Also, gambling was supposed to have destroyed me. Not so – I gamble and I win. What these suckers are trying to do is to apply standard formula to me and it just doesn't work.

Anyhow, long live the *NYQ*! And keep those editorials going! You're going to miss some invites to literary tea parties and even some of the established poets are going to look at you with askance, but doesn't it feel *good* to shake that rotten structure just a bit? [★ ★ ★]

---

1. Packard's novel, *Saturday Night at San Marcos*, published in 1985 by Thunder's Mouth Press, New York and reprinted in 1987 by Grove Press.
2. Bukowski married Linda Lee Beighle on August 18, 1985.

[To William Packard]
late October, 1985

[★ ★ ★] Got into a giant speed duel with some asshole on the Pasadena Freeway, this morning, the 3 bottle of Gamay Beaujolais hangover rising from my balls and out of the top of my Villon head, I got it up to 85 on the Devil's Curve where meat and bone are often separated in a flash of flaming nothingness and he fell back gasping, shifting down from 5th to 4th and flashing his front headlights in surrender. That'll teach 'em to fuck with a Suicide. [★ ★ ★]

[To John Martin]
December 11, 1985

Sometimes I wish I were this old guy sitting on the mountaintop subsisting on berries, grasshoppers or whatever. I wouldn't have to deal with the glazed eyes and lying dullness of my fellows, but I've got to admit I'm a sucker for modern plumbing and the racetrack.

Well, I've built my own little dungheap and here I sit flinging the shit about. There are minor and major regrets. And it's a hell of a thing to say but – I never met another man I'd rather be. And even if that's a delusion, it's a lucky one.

• 1986 •

[To Al Berlinsky]
January 8, 1986

[★ ★ ★] my home life here has developed into nightmare proportions. I'm unable to write about this portion of my life now and may never be able to but if I ever get the space to, I've got a novel that will make *Post Office, Factotum* and *Ham on Rye* look like kindergarten stuff. Some people seem to envision me floating in an easy dream world now . . . If they only knew . . .

Well, the damned gods have always liked to play with me . . . I'm one of their favorite toys.

[To William Packard]
January 28, 1986

You took five poems, and no matter how long I've been in the game, it was a lift to me, a *high* lift. And it came when really needed – other factors in my life have been fucking me over (you won't get a list here, I imagine you get enough dirty laundry from the poets).

. . . I went back to that hotel not too long ago and it's still there, although my buddy the desk clerk is no longer about, I can see the window that I hung out of one night by my ankles, I can still see it from the alley, and looking up at that fourth floor again, I can almost feel the same mad young rush of blood that was there, up and down the arms, and the whirling in the brain, I almost feel young again, like when closing the bars each night and sometimes coming out of them with a drunken female gazelle seemed the ultimate meaning and the ultimate victory.

Now they hustle drugs out of that place, it's murderous and dark and the cops don't go in there anymore. [★ ★ ★]

[To William Packard]
February 23, 1986

Thanks for your good letter. I don't know what the hell has happened to me of late: I used to tilt with adversity with a little more class than I have been showing. I think it finally becomes a matter of *wear*. Part of what is left of me has this odd dream of peace, not a total peace but bits and pieces of peace. It just doesn't happen. So I'm just going to have to toss out the dream and just work with the remains.

I think we all have to juggle and adjust our concepts as we go along. I just had a hard bad run of having to wade through shit that hardly seemed of my making. Although one can't always be sure of this. Just being alive seems to qualify us for whatever is about.

Anyhow, things seem better now. I'm on keel. And that's fair and good. I've always been one of these souls who is generally just about at a gentle ease under all the sundry conditions. It doesn't take much to make me happy and it takes very little, maybe almost nothing, maybe nothing, to make me contented. Small things please me, and at my worst I seldom feel anger, only disgust.

And the writing, like an old buddy, always seems to be there for me. When I'm down the most I get one kind of writing, when I'm contented – another. And when I'm happy, still yet another kind of writing.

The writing isn't everything but it counts. I also use racetrack therapy. Yesterday I pulled in $313.00. It's not the money but the money, I'll admit, is a balm when the royalties are slow. The track is more for forgetting and for working magic tricks. To get your horse to come in first is much like controlling part of the universe – like you have an inside hand on the forces. And you tend to forget a lot of petty shit that is whirling in your brain. We are eaten up by the hundreds of trivial things we have to do daily. Of course, you can just stay in bed and damn well get away from much of that, and I do *that* sometimes too. [★ ★ ★]

Everything is a matter of knowing, calmness and pace. Betting the horses lends me the ability to put a line down the way I like it . . ., want it. Each race is a war, a crisis, a finality, a result and a readjustment. The typer is the clarifier. I can understand why Hemingway watched the bullfights: it was the working of the scene. We seem to have to remind ourselves.

When I hear some people talking I am confounded with how far away they are from anything. Most of them speak what they have been taught, not what they have learned. And what they lack most are two things: gamble and humor. Especially the poets. The poets are the worst. But hell, I suppose if I were mainly a painter I'd say that the painters are the worst.

Anyhow, I feel pretty good tonight, sitting here drinking this wine and listening to Bach, and I think I've bailed myself out of the dark for a while. And my 5 cats and my wife and the walls soothe me, smooth me. That Bach, he was a mother-fucker, what?

[To John Martin]
Late June, 1986

> Whether my writing gets better or worse –
> You are my first hero and you remain that.
> We both started hard and low and we kept fighting.
> Never worry about my loyalty.

And please realize that any last word about anything *except* Sunday trivia – is *mine*.

I'm so happy that you're taking Julie[1] to Santa Rosa.

Please tell her that she can't fool me: I *know* she's *wonderful*!!

[To John Martin]
July 21, 1986

Well, it's not up to a writer to tell a publisher-editor how to run his business but since I was the one who brought Fante out of obscurity by continuously pointing to the neglect done to him . . .

I am now the one to tell only *you* that the way you keep bringing out books of his found under the mattress or wherever the hell are a great disservice to J.F. (I note a new Hemingway book out now, 25 years after his death.)

---

1. Julie Voss, Black Sparrow Press publisher's assistant from 1984 to 1991.

To publish the bad writing of great writers is much like beating the shit out of a man when he is totally drunk. It just ain't fair, baby.

Joyce Fante wrote me recently about a Fante book you had published. She wanted to know what I thought of it. As kindly as possible, I had to tell her.

Well, business is business, I suppose, and if a name moves a book it will be published.

and, Christ, like in Fante's awful screenwriting life, I too will be absent from the general wars for a while. There are certain re-write problems with *Barfly*, I mean, I have to go over it and fix it up, one total character in particular, but I think Barber has a good eye and I don't want to leave him in the lurch. At least I'm working on my own shit . . .

But if you don't hear from me for a while, understand, I am propping up the *Barfly*.

And I look forward to the release of *You Get So Alone*. The more I think of the title the more it works for me.

Hope this letter hasn't spoiled your day. Writers can get awful bitchy. Bad times on the homefront here make me a little edgy. Just want you to know that you are the greatest singular force that has kept me going. And how.

[To John Martin]
August 12, 1986

Thanks for the good letter. I don't think it hurts, sometimes, to remember where you came from. You know the places where I came from. Even the people who try to write about that or make films about it, they don't get it right. They call it "9 to 5." It's never 9 to 5, there's no free lunch break at those places, in fact, at many of them in order to keep your job you don't take lunch. Then there's *overtime* and the books never seem to get the overtime right and if you complain about *that*, there's another sucker to take your place.

You know my old saying, "Slavery was never abolished, it was only extended to include all the colors."

And what hurts is the steadily diminishing humanity of those fighting to hold jobs they don't want but fear the alternative worse. People simply empty out. They are bodies with fearful and obedient minds. The color leaves the eye. The voice becomes ugly. And the body. The hair. The fingernails. The shoes. Everything does.

As a young man I could not believe that people could give their lives over to those conditions. As an old man, I still can't believe it. What do they do it for? Sex? TV? An automobile on monthly payments? Or children? Children who are just going to do the same things that they did?

Early on, when I was quite young and going from job to job I was foolish enough to sometimes speak to my fellow workers: "Hey, the boss can come in here at any moment and lay all of us off, just like that, don't you realize that?"

They would just look at me. I was posing something that they didn't want to enter their minds.

Now in industry, there are vast layoffs (steel mills dead, technical changes in other factors of the work place). They are layed off by the hundreds of thousands and their faces are stunned:

"I put in 35 years . . ."

"It ain't right . . ."

"I don't know what to do . . ."

They never pay the slaves enough so they can get free, just enough so they can stay alive and come back to work. I could see all this. Why couldn't they? I figured the park bench was just as good or being a barfly was just as good. Why not get there *first* before they put me there? Why wait?

I just wrote in disgust against it all, it was a relief to get the shit out of my system. And now that I'm here, a so-called professional writer, after giving the first 50 years away, I've found out that there are *other* disgusts beyond the system . . .

I remember once, working as a packer in this lighting fixture company, one of the packers suddenly said: "I'll never be free!"

One of the bosses was walking by (his name was Morrie) and he let out this delicious cackle of a laugh, enjoying the fact that this fellow was trapped for life.

So, the luck I finally had in getting out of those places, no matter how long it took, *has* given me a kind of joy, the jolly joy of the miracle. I now write from an old mind and an old body, long beyond the time when most men would ever think of continuing such a thing, but since I started so late I owe it to myself to continue, and when the words begin to falter and I must be helped up stairways and I can no longer tell a bluebird from a paperclip, I still feel that something in me is going to remember (no matter how far I'm gone) how I've come through the murder and the mess and the moil, to at least a generous way to die.

To not to have entirely wasted one's life seems to be a worthy accomplishment, if only for myself.

[To John Martin]
September 2, 1986

September? Where did it all go? Now the tax man wants his quarterly payment and I see the first fangs of Christmas. Last couple of days even my horses have been falling to their knees, and if not, losing all the photo finishes. Well, a certain amount of defeat is necessary but when it becomes habitual and something to wallow in, that's bad. There's this poet I know who brags about all his defeats. He loses at everything and is really not too bad a writer but everybody avoids him because he always has the hand out and screams and rages because he's not as famous as he thinks he should be. It bothers him. That's one loss he doesn't want to take. If he typed as much as he complained maybe he'd be luckier. And he badmouths the work of others. He finally got lucky and was taken in by this lady who attempted to fix him up. Fed and clothed him, got up a brochure for him, lined up a string of poetry readings. He decided to make it. Get it straight. An editor I know wrote to me, "I hope he doesn't blow it . . ." This poet is *loud* and over-demanding.

Well, he blew it. Last I heard he was heading toward San Diego and he looked like hell. Stopped here in town, got some money from a bookseller and wanted to know my phone number. Said bookseller was wise enough not to give.

Maybe I'm too hard on this poet. He could be a mental case. I've been to the track with him. He bets 99-to-one shots and after it's all over he says, "Well, fuck, you can't beat the game."

You do more work in one day than he does in a year.

It's true that the fates are unkind and will finally make mush of all of us, but there's nothing more tiring than the good, immortal loser. The secret is that anybody can lose, it's the easiest talent.

I'll have to say that the best thing that happened to me this year was something that never happened: picking up the phone and hearing his voice. I may be my brother's keeper, but not on *demand*.

[To John Martin]
September 26, 1986

Still hell on the battlefront and the poem is still the easiest way out of hell but went back to the story in spite of it all. After all, too many excuses can be made for not doing things, for not doing anything, in fact.

And still, I feel the itch and need to do another novel but don't quite know how to land on the material. My god, I may still find a circular way.

I note the good luck on the recent check, and also of the news on *Women*, which is certainly good. I realize, that on the contract (I haven't read it) that there might be a certain percentage due you, due me, on all this. Since you have negotiated and worked hard on this matter, of course, you will get the agent's fee. And if you think there should be more (I mean, agent's fee *plus* what it now says in the contract), please let me know.

We've always had a marvelous way of getting along; I don't think we've had one bad argument or a disruption of feelings in our two decades together. Whether we realize it or not, I think this has made you a better editor-publisher and has helped make me a better writer.

I must guess that you've caught plenty of shit from the poets and the critics and the poet-critics for publishing me but you've gone ahead anyhow.

And from my part, I've gotten plenty of anti-John Martin flak at this end. You should hear some of the bitter and bitching stories and opinions I get at this end. Most of this, I don't respond to. To the few I say, "Even if true, whatever he did, he did for a reason and the reason wasn't against me, it was for his survival and he needed that."

They don't realize how many publishers have gone under, how each edge must be fought for constantly and daily. They don't realize that you must be a bill collector, a book collector, a reader of manuscripts and often a shipping clerk and a truck loader, and a cheer-leader to your own small staff. And they don't realize that each book you publish is a gamble on your *own* survival, your continuance. Also, they don't realize the many things you have done for me which have kept me going when I might have not kept going. By this, I mean the monies given outright, and the mass of work and arrangement done to submit my crap to the various university archives.

And all the work done on the archives, the hours and hours, the order, the perfect letters to the librarians, the fitting of the pages in order, the shipping of such, and all the other attendant worries. And all this without *any* financial reward to you. (financail?) (never could spell) (make it financial)

I guess I'm saying all this because of my age: being 66 lends some doubt; I'd hate like hell to be running in a one hundred yard dash.

The writing must slip, surely has, although it feels better than ever to me. But the seas of booze I have consumed must leave their mark, plus the attendant years.

So, I want to say these good thoughts I have of you while I am still able to. The way I drink on certain nights of unhappiness might take me out or lead to stroke, so I better say a few things now.

But, all and all, I figure I'm just going to get better and better at writing, right up to the lip of the grave. It's just a feeling.

Of course, there are other things more important than writing. But it's all I know. And what a glorious hell of a "know," what a crazy grand way to face the impossible.

Long live the Sparrow!

[To John Martin]
near Thanksgiving, 1986

Well, yes, we've got to be thankful that somewhere our words were finally heard and that we didn't have to dilute them to get the luck. And maybe we've fought where others might have quit. It's hard to know. I only did what something drove me to do. Take a pit bull: once he clamps those jaws you've got to use a megaforce of total unbelievable, non-measurable searing leaping hell hell hell to make him let go. Yet that pit-bull is not doing anything exceptional, he's only doing what he was set-up to do. He has no other way, no other choice.

There are no brave men. There are only men who pretend to be brave. Or women. Or hawks.

I have regrets. Like, even now, as the luck might hold tenderly, there's never any real peace. Things keep gnawing, grinding, looming. Death I've long been ready for, somehow she seems a sweet Bitch. But – I get soft, maybe always have been, still yearn for that ultimate magic that could be there in some *other* person. I think that's the saddest of the sad, but maybe I've got it coming. The non-connect, I mean. Maybe the gods figure that anything near-pleasant might destroy the concentration on the pit bull grip-within this game.

Sounds like a lot of crap and probably is.

With the writing though, I always feel the same: I am beginning at a beginning and moving through, against and with it. I am the same now as I was when I first started writing. It's a grand show, no credit accepted, but the sound of this machine like the sound of all the others, it's a functional joy that doesn't seem to relent, and accidental, meant or just irrational, I'll take it, take it, take it.

[To Gerald Locklin]
November 21, 1986

Thanks for fine poem in recent *Wormie*, I mean the one explaining to the disclaimers why I might do as I do. Actually, I have heard bitchings and wailings about what I do or don't do or what I should do since about the time I wrote my first poem. I think since my writing is open-mannered, people feel freer in discussing it and me. I've long grown used to this and feel that without the rantings and complaints of the sometimes envious I might even feel let down.

In *Barfly*, Mickey Rourke and Fay Dunaway are to play the leads. And when the lead actor gets 750 times what the writer does, there might be a tendency not to listen to the writer but I speak anyhow and will continue to suggest basic things. One thing I *do have going* is that not a line of the script can be changed without my O.K. This, thanks to Barbet Schroeder, director. I've made certain revisions for the camera's eye but all in all the whole bit runs too long and cutting is just like cutting off parts of your body but I suppose it must be done.

Mailer works for Cannon also. Met him at his place and we had some drinks. "Norman," I told him, "Hollywood scares the shit out of me."

He just looked at me like I didn't quite know what I was saying.

Oh yeah, when I met him we shook hands and I said, "The Barfly meets the Heavyweight Champ." He liked that.

Shooting starts sometime in January and I've already told the people that I won't be able to be there on the days the horses are running. Actually, I will be glad to get back to the poem and the short story. I've turned down a couple of screenplay offers. The money is there but I dislike the media much; most movies repulse me and I remember what happened to Fante: Hollywood killed him. I don't need that kind of money – the old BMW is at 130,000 miles and running fine. Had it since 1979. The main thing is to get the word down the way you have to. Lose that and no bankroll in the world can get it back for you. [★ ★ ★]

Actually, the best thing to come out of this movie thing is *The Bukowski Tapes*. I felt sorry for Barbet because he paid me to write *Barfly*, wrote it in 1979 and felt like he would never get rid of it, so I got drunk for many days, many hours, many nights and talked with the camera on me. He got *four hours* worth of tapes which he is going to bring out in video. I think I babbled pretty lucky and pretty wild and have enclosed a list of the tales from the wine bottle for your bemusement.

But, as you know, the typewriter is the only place to work from. These poets who call themselves *performance artists* are only trying to fancy up their petty vanities. The whole reading circuit is a mass of dismal dull crap. [★ ★ ★]

[To John Martin]
December 19, 1986

[★ ★ ★] On *Barfly*, there's still to be more tinkering with the script. Minor technical changes, also cuts because it runs too long and they don't have that kind of money; also cuts because too expensive and complicated to shoot certain scenes. If I had known this from the beginning I would have set the whole thing up in the bar, a la stage play. Of course, then they would have said, show us something of his life outside the bar.

What they are doing is *worrying* the thing to death.

I told Barbet, if they had just shot the thing as I originally wrote it, they would have had a better thing than what they have now.

"Oh no!" he said.

What they are doing is thinking of other movies, of standard ways and processes. That's bad. What you do is shoot the raw material as is and people feel and appreciate that. The last thing they want is finesse. The natural fibre is what invigorates.

Well, supposedly, they begin shooting Jan. 19 and I'll be free of their strictures. And I hope, of course, that the money comes through. [★ ★ ★]

INDEX

Alcatraz 189
Altrice, Janice 67
Anderson, Sherwood 185, 196
Anthology of L. A. Poets, An 23
Aunt Harriet's Flair for Writing Review 57

Bach, Johann Sebastian 57, 75, 207
Barfly 118, 127, 132, 138, 143, 147, 156, 178, 208, 213, 214
Beighle, Linda Lee 95, 96, 97, 99, 102, 106–7, 108, 110, 112, 115, 117, 118, 119, 120, 121, 122, 125, 126, 127, 130, 133, 134, 135, 136, 141, 142, 143, 144–5, 146, 149, 155, 157, 159, 166, 173, 180, 202
Bellow, Saul 173, 186
Berlinsky, Al 184–5, 205
Berryman, John 19
Black Sparrow Press 5, 13, 26, 68, 70, 77, 95, 114, 133, 144, 157, 161, 183, 190, 196, 199, 207, 212
Blaufuss, Bix 10
Blazek, Douglas 1, 61, 165
Blue Book, The 188
Bogart, Humphrey 61, 95, 138
Brahms, Johannes 70
Brandes, Pamela 84–6, 88, 90
Braun, Eva 129
Bronstein, Lynne 67
Bruckner, Anton 75, 180
Bukowski, Charles:
    art, discusses nature of 7, 22, 26, 30, 37, 198–9
    depression 12, 13, 16–17, 54, 140, 156
    drinking 4, 7, 9, 15, 39–41, 46, 47–8, 49, 56, 71, 72, 74, 76, 77, 82, 88, 94, 97, 101, 102, 107, 108, 109, 111, 112, 115, 116, 117, 119, 125, 127, 129, 134, 135, 138, 140, 141, 143, 144–5, 146, 152, 155, 157, 158, 159, 160, 163, 165, 166, 168–9, 171, 177–8, 181, 184, 186, 188, 190, 200, 201, 202, 212, 214
    family 25, 28, 35, 91 *see also* Beighle, Linda Lee
    finances 1, 3, 5, 6, 8, 9, 20, 26, 27, 28, 34, 40, 47, 51, 57, 66, 77, 87, 89, 91, 102, 103, 112, 120, 121, 122, 126, 129, 130, 131, 132–3, 134, 135–6, 139, 143–4, 156, 157, 158–9, 168, 173, 177, 191, 197, 206, 213
    gambling 144, 146, 161, 171, 173, 181, 190, 197, 203, 206
    health 20, 45–6, 47, 116, 145, 165, 175–6, 200, 213
    jobs 12, 149, 209
    literary influences 2, 14, 16, 17, 19, 30, 31, 43, 44, 47, 49, 56, 58–9, 61, 62, 63, 67, 68, 69, 70, 71, 72, 73, 79, 82, 86, 87, 88, 92, 95, 99, 100, 109–10, 111, 112, 116, 122–3, 126, 127–8, 134–5, 139, 144, 150–1, 158, 168, 171, 172, 173, 174–5, 185, 186, 189, 193, 194, 196, 197, 199, 200, 207
    loner 9, 149–51, 157–8, 162, 171
    poetry 5, 7, 9, 10, 15, 19, 23–4, 32, 36, 41, 51, 55, 57, 62, 67–8, 80–2, 93, 95, 99, 101, 102, 106, 113, 129, 130, 136–7, 138, 143, 144, 145, 147, 152, 157, 162–3, 165–6, 168, 171, 177–9, 187,

188, 190, 191, 205, 207, 210–11, 213
public appearances, readings 2, 36, 40–1, 66, 93, 107, 111, 125, 128–9, 136–7, 143, 144–5, 160, 161, 179, 193, 210
screenplays and movies see *Barfly* and Hollywood
women 2, 3–4, 5, 6, 7, 8, 10, 12, 14, 15–16, 19, 20, 21–2, 24, 27–33, 34, 35, 36–40, 42, 44, 45–6, 47, 50, 52, 53, 54, 63, 64–5, 69, 74, 75, 76, 77, 80–2, 83, 84–6, 87, 89, 90, 91–2, 94, 95, 96, 97, 99, 100, 102, 106–7, 108, 109, 110, 112, 115, 117, 118, 119, 120, 121, 122, 125, 126–7, 130, 133, 134, 135, 136–7, 141, 142, 143, 144–5, 146, 149, 155, 157, 159, 160, 166, 169, 171, 174, 179, 180, 183–4
works *see under individual name*
Bukowski, Marina (daughter) 118–19
Bukowski: Friendship, Fame & Bestial Myth (Sherman) 179
Bukowski Tapes, The 214
Bull, Joanna 45, 52–3
Burroughs, William 193
By Land, Sea & Air 168

Cagney, James 94
Cain, James M. 185
California Bicentennial Poets Anthology 72
California School of Psychology 52
Capote, Truman 116, 200
Catullus 79, 168
Céline, Louis-Ferdinand 2, 30, 73, 109, 112, 151, 158, 185, 197, 199
Charles Bukowski Spit in My Face (Barker) 179
Charles Bukowski: A Comprehensive Checklist 1946–1982 (Fogel) 170
Chatterton, Thomas 16
Cherry, Neeli 1, 6, 13–14, 23, 151
Christoferson, Chris 147
City Lights 3, 22, 27, 34, 95, 102, 128, 132, 143

Clark, Tom 69
Connell, Patricia 27–33, 34, 35, 36–40
Corrington, William 125–6, 156, 166
Creeley, Robert 13, 46
Creem 67
Crucifix in a Deathhand 155
Cummings, e. e. 199, 200

Dallas Cowboys 56
Dangerfield, Rodney 170
Derschau, Renate 106
Detroit Free Press 66
Di Fonzi 133, 138, 143
Dickey, James 56, 102, 194
Dillinger, John 141, 196
Dostoevsky, Fyodor 30
Dunaway, Fay 213
Dustbooks from Paradise 50

Eliot, T. S. 200
Eshleman, Clayton 47, 100

Faulkner, William 127–8, 175
Ferlinghetti, Lawrence 3, 13, 29, 69, 95, 121, 122, 128, 131
Ferrie, Marco 163, 166
Fett, Heinrich 96, 108
Fitzgerald, F. Scott 8, 59
Fitzgerald, Zelda 8
Flower, Fist and Bestial Wail 12, 144
Flynt, Larry 109, 121
Fogel, Al 158–9, 170, 175–6, 190
Fool, The 177
Ford, Henry 76
Ford, Robert 76
Fox, Hugh 25, 26, 27, 59
Frost, Robert 200
Fuck Machine 128

Gazzara, Ben 163, 166, 184
Ginsberg, Allen 51, 69, 119, 162, 193
Glière, Reinhold Moritzovich 75
Godard, Jean-Luc 160
Gogol, Nikolay 174
Gold, Mike 165
Goodwin, Douglas 185–6
Graham, Billy 111

217

Griffith, E. V. 12–13
Grosz, George 142

Hackford, Taylor 71
Ham On Rye 161, 163, 167, 171, 197, 205
Hamsun, Knut 43, 109, 134, 199
Hardy, Thomas 134
Harrison, Jim 58
Hatchetman Press 1
Hemingway, Ernest 16, 51, 59, 70, 72, 88, 95, 144, 185, 207
Hi-times 177
Hitler, Adolf 95, 172, 197
Hollywood 23–4, 82, 138, 157, 159, 166, 213–14
Holy Doors: An Anthology of Poetry, Prose and Criticism 25, 45
Home Planet News 168
Hope, Bob 76, 111
Hustler 88, 109, 121, 123

Islands in the Stream (Hemingway) 51

Jack the Ripper 95
'Jockey, The' 175
Johnson, Lyndon 46
Journey (Celine) 2
Juarez, Ebenezer 57

Kafka, Franz 30, 63
Kelly, Robert 43
Kenyon Review 23
Kessler, Stephen 189, 191, 192
King, Linda 21–2, 24, 33, 35, 36, 37–9, 41, 45, 47, 50, 51, 52, 53, 54, 69, 77, 83, 100, 106, 169, 174
Kitty Foyle (Morley) 63
Klopp, Karyl 74
Kosinski, Jerzy 34

L.A. Times 80
L.A. Free Press 2, 67–8, 87
Lamantia, Philip 50
Laugh Literary and Man the Humping Guns 1, 14, 23, 62, 165
Lawrence, D. H. 150

Laxness, Halldor 22
Leithauser, Brad 22
Lewis, Sinclair 175
Life and Death in a Charity Ward 95
Locklin, Gerald 3, 56, 127, 142, 159–61, 162, 167, 168, 171–2, 173–5, 177–9, 186–7, 213
London Magazine 95
Longfellow, Henry Wadsworth 68
Los Angeles 23–4
'Lost Generation, The' 185

Mahler, Gustav 75
Mailer, Norman 92, 116, 172, 173, 186, 213
Malanga, Gerard 41–2
Malone, Hank 8–9, 71, 72, 93–4, 97, 109, 111, 113, 142–3, 161, 184
Man Who Loved Women, The 102
Mann, Thomas 134
Maronick, Gregory 15–17
Martin, Barbara 20, 44, 62, 70, 71, 75, 77, 78, 134, 150
Martin, John 1, 2, 3–4, 5, 6, 7, 8, 11, 13, 14–15, 17, 20, 22–4, 26, 41, 43, 46, 47, 49, 50, 53, 62, 63, 65, 66, 69, 70, 75, 77, 78, 79, 80, 83, 86–7, 89, 91, 93, 95–6, 98, 101, 102, 103, 105, 107, 111, 112, 113–15, 120–1, 129–31, 132–4, 135–6, 137–41, 143–4, 147, 149–51, 156–8, 169–70, 180, 183, 190–1, 195–6, 198–9, 203, 207–13, 214–15
Marx, Karl 61
Marx, Zippo 76
Mason & Lipscomb 79
Maugham, Somerset 52, 63
McCullers, Carson 68
McKuen, Rod 15, 68, 102
Mencken, H. L. 111, 189
Micheline, Jack 54, 55, 59, 92, 100, 115
Michener, James A. 173
Miller, Henry 82, 122–3, 126, 150, 151, 158, 185, 193
Miller, Larry 82, 126
Monroe, Marilyn 64, 65

Montfort, Michael 117, 119, 121, 126, 128, 131, 133, 196
More, Koko (Schroeder) 118
Mozart, Wolfgang Amadeus 108

Namath, Joe 76
New York Quarterly 7, 116, 135, 143, 161, 189, 194, 196, 197, 202
New York Review of Books 22
New York Times 71
Nicholson, Jack 146
Nietzsche, Friedrich 22
90 Minutes in Hell 97
NOLA 2, 3–4, 59
Nomades 129–30
Norse, Harold 10, 50–1, 53, 59, 60

Onion Field, The 138, 143
Other Side, The 2
Outsider 125
Owen, Wilfred 197

Packard, William 7, 51, 116, 122–3, 134–5, 136–7, 144–6, 187–8, 194–5, 196, 197–8, 199, 200, 202, 203, 205, 206–7
Passionate Years, The (Crosby) 185
Patchen, Kenneth 10, 19
Pavilion of Women (Buck) 108
Penguin Contemporary Poets 50
Peters, Nancy 122
Picasso, Pablo 49
Pitts, Jimmy 3
Playboy 102, 103
Pleasants, Ben 2
Plymell, Charles 75–6
Poetry Now 67, 69
Polanski, Roman 139
Pomegranate Press 74
Portrait of the Artist as a Young Man, A (Joyce) 76
Post Office 2, 13, 15, 30, 34, 66, 95, 205
Pound, Ezra 44, 49, 56, 58, 87, 99, 109, 174, 199
Proust, Marcel 194

Racing Form 76

Rape Rope 139
Rats of Thirst, The 129, 132–3
Rebel, The (Camus) 55
Richmond, Steve 13–14, 25, 26, 27, 31, 57, 58, 100, 101
Robson, William J. 25–6
Rogue 26
Rolling Stone 67, 75, 86
Rourke, Mickey 213

Saroyan, William 73, 185
Schopenhauer, Arthur 139
Schroeder, Barbet 118, 123, 127, 128, 131, 132, 138, 143, 147, 160, 213, 214
Second Coming 23, 45
Sedricks, Andre 10
Septuagenarian Stew 175
Sesar, Carl 79
7 on Style 62, 64
Shakespeare Never Did This 117, 131, 138, 143
Sibelius, Jean 135
Sloman, Larry 'Ratso' 181
Small Press Review 50, 58
Stangos, Nikos 50
Stapen, Joe 152–3, 162–3
Stein, Gertrude 17
Steinbeck, John 173
Stern 106, 108
Streetwalker 177
Sweet and Dirty 47–8
Sybionese Liberation Army 60–1

Tales of Ordinary Madness 163, 166–7, 178, 184
Terror Street 65
Thomas, Dylan 16, 86
Thurber, James 4, 88, 187
Time 75
Truffaut, François 102
Truman, Harry 44, 46
Turgenev, Ivan 185
TV and Fine Arts Guide 51

U.C.L.A. 19
University of Arizona 29, 32, 39

University of Arkansas 9
University of California 1, 5
University of Chicago Library 6
University of Kansas 10
University of Wisconsin 9
USA (Dos Passos) 87

Vagabond 6
Van Gogh, Vincent 16
Vangelisti, Paul 23
Vietnam War 71
Voltrout 119, 121, 126, 133
Voss, Julie 207

Wagner, Richard 74
Wakoski, Diane 14
Wantling, Ruthie 62, 64, 98
Webb, Jon 15, 51, 70, 125–6, 155, 166, 176
Webb, Louise 70, 125–6, 155, 156, 166–7, 176
Weissner, Carl 3, 4–5, 7, 10, 19, 21–2, 24–5, 34, 36, 40–2, 47–8, 54, 55, 60–1, 63–5, 66, 71–2, 74, 82, 88, 90, 94, 95, 96, 97, 98, 101, 102, 103, 105–7, 108, 110, 111–13, 115, 117, 118, 119, 120, 121, 122, 126–7, 128–30, 131, 132–4, 135–6, 138, 142, 145, 190–1, 196

Western Avenue 138
Whitaker, James 57–8
White Heat 94
Whitman, Walt 197
Wilkofsky, Roth 74, 75
Williams, Liza 28, 29, 30, 32, 33, 34, 35, 36, 37, 38, 40, 64
Williams, William Carlos 58
Winans, A. D. 23, 45, 48, 49, 50, 51, 53–4, 55, 56, 58–60, 62, 63, 69, 72–3, 87, 88–90, 91–2, 95, 99–100, 101, 102, 116, 146
'With Rue My Heart Is Laden' (Housman) 116
Wolfe, Thomas 100, 158
Women 79, 83, 87, 89, 91, 93, 98, 100, 101, 102, 105, 107, 109, 113, 114–15, 119, 120, 122–3, 126, 127, 129, 134, 138, 142, 143
Woods, James 138, 143
Woolf, Douglas 100
Wormwood 135, 160, 213

Yevtushenko, Yevgeny 36, 128
You Get So Alone at Times That It Just Makes Sense 185, 208
Young, Lafayette 2, 3, 25

Zweitauserdeins 196